In Christ....walking by Grace and Faith

14-week Inductive Bible study of the book of Ephesians

by Mandi Cornett

In Christ....walking by Grace and Faith
Copyright@2013 by Mandi Cornet

Table of Contents

EPHESIANS THOUGHTS

To think that we could plumb the depths of one of the most theologically intricate books of the New Testament in 14 weeks would be absolutely insane! We will barely scratch the surface. "I know," you say, "but it's 14 weeks!" I'll tell you up front that we won't be able to dive into everything. There is so much to be gleaned. Feel free to use this study as a jumping-off point for your own deeper study. Please know that God laid this particular study on my heart in 2004 and He wouldn't allow me to let it go.

With lots of prayer, faith, and grace, we are going to head into the book of Ephesians together, asking God specifically and exactly what Paul asked for in Ephesians 1:18a, "that the eyes of our hearts would be enlightened" by Him. He has so much that He wants to teach, challenge, encourage, strengthen, and change in us. That's not all—there is also so much power and blessing that He wants to bestow on us, His beloved, by the power of His Holy Spirit, and by the study of His Word. We can never get too much of His truth this side of eternity.

Ephesians is a wonderful book in the New Testament and a personal favorite of mine! This study may be too easy for many of you, and for many of you it may be too much. As with any of my studies, don't get bogged down with the homework. The homework is designed to get you into the Word and thinking. If you don't know me well, I'm a big fan of thinking! It's okay to not understand it all, and if a question just doesn't make sense, skip it. (Before you skip it, if you pretend you hear me saying it, it might help.) If there is not enough "meat" to the homework, then by all means dig deeper and come to study! Just get into the Word and start thinking! Meditate, ponder and pray on it....consider joining with a friend to discuss.

Please make sure you use the copy of the book of Ephesians in the back of your study. I study and write from the New American Standard Version of the Bible, and you will be confused by the questions about the book if you don't use it. Please feel free to use your own version for cross-references, but when you do your homework and the question is from Ephesians, it will help to use this text (and you can write all over it!). Learn to "think" on the paper. I've added **Ponder*** spots in the homework; they are a series of questions to just think on (ponder). Don't feel you have to answer all of them. They are just to get you thinking.

My sisters, you are loved and I'm so excited to share this time with you. May the Lord change each of us by the working of His Word! May not one of us be the same after we have delved into the book of Ephesians together. May we see Him and His purposes more clearly and may we love what He loves more and more until we see Him face-to-face!

Anticipating what He wants to do,
Mandi

www.cleansefillpour.com
Contact email- cleansefillpour@aol.com

WEEK 1
Birdseye View with Bookends
Book of Ephesians

The book of Ephesians was written by the apostle Paul to the believers at Ephesus. He had been in Ephesus for two years, sharing the gospel and strengthening the church in that region. He left Timothy there to support, pastor, and help the elders.

Paul loved this group of believers, he loved the Lord, and he loved the truth of the message of the gospel of Jesus Christ. He wanted to see all of these believers grow to become working parts of the body of Christ. He wanted them to realize what they truly had "in Christ." Hold on to your hats; Ephesians is an exciting book!!

After an introductory lecture, hopefully you have a handle on the context of the "when" and the "who" of the book of Ephesians. This week we are going to look at a broad overview of the book. But first, let's look at Paul's last face-to-face meeting with the elders at Ephesus before his imprisonment in Rome (where he wrote this letter).

Let's look at some history and how Ephesians fits together in the New Testament. We'll look at two places; think of them as "bookends." Yes, bookends. This is the first bookend that happened *before* the book of Ephesians was written.

Week 1—Day 1

Read Acts 20:17–38. This event takes place **before** the book of Ephesians is written. Think through and answer these questions:

1. How would you describe Paul's heart for this church in Ephesus?

2. What is his concern for them? What does he say will eventually happen in the church at Ephesus?

3. Can you see a direct warning to them? What is it?

4. Think through these verses. Paul knows he is going to jail and will not see them again, yet he is concerned about them. What does this say about his heart for the Lord?

5. Where has he placed his hope, even when he has NO control? Support your answer from the text.

This passage (Acts 20) is a specific address to the leadership (elders). The book of Ephesians is written to ALL the saints. As you read the book, keep in mind his warning to the elders in Acts 20 and start processing/thinking about why Paul would write about the specific things he does in the book of Ephesians.

Now, let's take a look at a passage **after** the book of Ephesians was written. This is the other side of the "bookend."
Look at Revelation 2:1–7. This strategic church, the church in Ephesus, is mentioned in Revelation sixty plus years **after** the book of Ephesians was written. See if you glean any thoughts. What ended up happening there? How were Paul's concerns (remember what he said sixty plus years *earlier* to the elders) confirmed?

As you read through Ephesians this week, which is in the middle (what is in between the bookends!), remember who the people of this church were. Remember these were real people, in a real place—with a huge responsibility being in a strategic place both geographically and historically. This church is part of the first-century church. The foundation is being laid for you and me.

Ponder*
What foundation are we laying for future generations? What kind of foundation are we laying for our children and grandchildren? Will our foundation be strong? Is Jesus our first love? Do we

really know Him and what He has done for us? Are you excited yet? Let's dig into Ephesians, the book in between the "bookends"!

Week 1—Days 2 and 3

Take a couple of days and read the entire book of Ephesians (use the text that we gave you in the back). Start thinking and examining Paul's flow of thought. Write down what you think his main point is; in other words, what is he talking about or what does he seem to emphasize? In each of these segments below, jot down simple, general thoughts. Pray before you begin, and then let your mind start digging into this great book. Don't over think. We are putting the corner and edge pieces of the puzzle of Ephesians together. (First bookends, now puzzles!) There are no right or wrong answers—just observations. What does he want them to understand in these segments? Please just list a *few* thoughts.

Segment 1   1:3–2:10

Segment 2   2:11–3:13

Segment 3   3:14–21

Segment 4   4–6:9

Segment 5   6:10–24

Week 1—Days 4 and 5

Read over the book again and mark these words (in your own way, draw a circle around the word or a square, whatever!) and think about what you learn about this word and this phrase.

Walk

In the heavenly/in the heavenly places

Write down your thoughts or just think and pray about the following.

1. What do you think of when you hear the word "walk"?

2. Can you think of some examples of what "the walk" Paul is talking about might look like today for you and me?

3. What exactly is in the "heavenly places"?

4. Where are the heavenly places?

Remember; don't be frustrated if you have more questions than you do answers. Praise the Lord that you are thinking! Actually, that is a good thing!
Hopefully, you did all of this in several sittings and now you have read the entire book a couple of times. Next week we'll start digging into some specifics in chapter 1. Overviews are not my favorite, but they are necessary. Thank you for your diligence. Any time you spend learning God's truth is eternal and time well spent. He promises (Isa. 55:10–11)! Remember you are loved! He wants to meet with you!

WEEK 2
Change of Position "IN"
Ephesians 1:1–14

Last week was overview and it was relatively painless, right? This week we start to dig in! The concept of being "In Christ" is a powerful one, honestly, it has rocked my world! This truth is true because it is true. This truth changes how we look, not only at ourselves, but also how we see each other in the Body of Christ, and the lost and dying world. Out is out. Period. In is IN! Period. We were *all* born out of relationship with God, but by grace and faith in the life, death, burial and resurrection of Jesus Christ- by His finished work on the Cross…we can be brought in. That positional change, from out to IN, changes everything! I am praying for you, right now, as you dig into Ephesians 1.

Days 1 and 2

Read Ephesians 1:1–2. List who "the players" are in this letter. In other words, who is this written to and by whom?

Please reread Ephesians 1:3–2:10. Get the feel for the direction that Paul is headed. Once again, what do you think is his main point/points? What does Paul seem to be focusing on or talking about?

Let's take a close-up look at just the beginning. Honestly, this little section (to me) is the most difficult and wordy section of the whole book! Can you believe that is where we have to start?! Look at 1:3–14 carefully. We are going to take some steps in handling this section.

Step 1
Circle the phrase "in Him" or "in Christ." Jot down what hits you.

Step 2

Reread 1:3–14. Read it through slowly and carefully. Try to figure out who the "Him" is: Is it referring to God or Jesus? Some are easier than others to catch, so don't spend too much time here; think it through. Is it God or Jesus who is being talked about? If you want to, you can mark each pronoun (God and Jesus) in a distinctive way so that you can see clearly which one is being talked about.

Ponder*

The real question is; *do you see* the relationship between God and Christ? God and us? Jesus and us? The Holy Spirit and us? Who is the *only* key to the relationship with God? Why is that important to understand?

It is vital that we see the relationship involved. God–Jesus–Spirit-us. Take a look at these references and see what the connection is between God and us. What is Jesus called or what has He done?

John 1:17–18 (watch the He/Him at the end of v. 18)—Who explained who?

John 14:6

Romans 5:1–2

1 Timothy 2:5–6

Hebrews 10:19–22

Week 2—Day 3

Obviously, Jesus is the only way to have a right relationship with God. We enter into that relationship when we see that we are lost in our sin and then believe or trust in what Jesus did for us by dying on the cross, in our place and for our sins. He was buried and then raised on the third day, which is the proof that His payment for sin was accepted. Yeah!!!

In other words, we are saved from our sin and forgiven when we trust in Jesus' finished work on our behalf (Eph. 2:8–9). We can't be in right standing with God on our own; no one can. We need to see our need and understand what Jesus did and put our trust in His finished work to save us; because of that, we can now be "in Christ." What is the result of being "in Christ"? What are the blessings/benefits besides eternal life after we die? How about the here and now? This passage is absolutely full of that truth. If you have been born into the family of God, you are "in Christ" and all these things are positionally yours. These things are yours because of your position "in Christ." Period. What things? Well, that is the next step.

Step 3

Read 1:3–14 and list the results of being "in Christ." What are you called/considered to be by Him? Simply write down what you learn from each verse. It is amazing! I'll give you hints. Again, this is a wordy passage, but we want to see what we have as believers or what we are called. Don't sweat it; just give it a try. I'll start you out by doing a couple of the difficult ones. You fill in the rest!

	Results of being in Christ	OR	What we are called as believers "in Christ"
v. 3	blessed us with every spiritual blessing in the heavenly places		
v. 4			
v. 4			
v. 4			
v. 5			
v. 6	have had His grace freely bestowed (KJV uses "accepted") on us in the Beloved		
v. 7			

v. 7

v. 8

v. 9   made known to us the mystery of His will

v. 11   have obtained an inheritance

v. 12   we would be to the praise of His glory

v. 13

v. 14

Do we really realize that this is *who we are* now? This is how the God of the universe looks at you! The first thing I say is, "Well, I certainly don't feel that way, nor look that way!" BUT this is *who I am* and *who you are* if we are "in Christ." Pick three of these benefits or blessings and think on them.

1.

2.

3.

Ponder*
What is hitting your heart? Why did you pick those particular benefits to think on? How do they affect your everyday life? How should they? If your perspective changed and you viewed these things as true about yourself, would your everyday life change? How?

In Christ, I have been "made accepted in the Beloved" (in this case, I love the King James Version!). I have struggled with feeling accepted for as long as I can remember. I'm not sure why. I had a loving home and a great foundation, but I never felt like I fit in. I had typical girl stuff and typical boy stuff, but even into my adulthood and marriage, I struggled. Then motherhood happened—that made it even worse! I felt like a square peg in a round hole—always looking for approval and never finding it, never feeling accepted.

This verse and a series of verses have taught me so much and have brought great healing to my heart. "In Christ," I am accepted. I belong. I fit. I have a place and I am accepted. Not because of me but because of Him. He brought me in. Whether I feel like it or not, the fact of the matter is, as a believer, I am accepted. If you have come to a personal relationship with Jesus Christ, by faith and grace alone, then you are accepted as well. I am not more accepted or less accepted than you—we are accepted. He has made you to be accepted, by His grace, in the Beloved. What a truth!!!

Week 2—Day 4

Before we jump into some word studies, re-read Ephesians 1:13-14 very slowly. Look closely at the pronouns used and then glance back up at the previous verses (3-12), what do you notice?

What is the difference between a personal pronoun and plural pronouns, meaning an individual "you" becoming a part of the corporate "we"? How did a "you" become a part of the "we"? What do you learn about the Gospel?

Let's do some word studies. The original language of the New Testament was Greek. Word studies are just looking at the original language for more insight into the word used. I've heard it said that English is like black and white, and that seeing the Greek is like looking at it in color. Language is a beautiful thing. Feel free to look up any words that look interesting to you.

Look up the following words in a regular dictionary or a Greek word study (I use the *Complete Word Study, New Testament*, by Dr. Zodhiates). Or you can go to Google, and enter the Strong's number that is in parenthesis. It takes some time but it's fun! I also have a glossary of words at the end of this study.

Write anything that brings to light Paul's use of the following words.

v. 5   adoption (Strong's #5206)

v. 7   redemption (#629)

v. 13   sealed (#4972)

v. 14   pledge (#728)

Are there any other words that strike you as interesting? Enlightening?

Week 2—Day 5

We are in a close familial relationship with the one true God! He knows all about us and He wants to be known by us—by you. Verse 9 says that we are to know the mystery of His will. Look up the word *know* (Strong's #1107). What do you learn?

How can we being to know and understand the mystery of His will if we don't *know* Him? Let's see what "price tag" Jesus puts on knowing God. How much does Jesus value us knowing Him?

Read John 17:3. This is Jesus' final prayer to the Father before He is handed over to die in our place. He prayed this for His disciples and for those who believe because of their word. That's you and me, sister!! He also prayed this for you and me. Think about it, how does Jesus define "eternal life"?

According to this verse, does that start when you die?

Does God want to be known? He sure does. We'll finish by looking at a few references and then add to these thoughts next week too.

Please look up these references about what kind of relationship the Lord desires and what He has made known. Let them speak to your heart. What do you learn?

Isaiah 43:1–7

Jeremiah 31:33–34

Romans 11:33–12:2

2 Peter 1:2–3

How about Paul? What are his thoughts about knowing God? Read Philippians 3:7–11.

My wonderful sister "in Christ," let's fall more and more in love with the One who not only made a way for us to be in relationship with Him but also wants us to know Him and understand His will! Keep digging. Seek truth, for it will be found. His truth is priceless, life changing, and eternal.

This is His will for you and for me: *to know Him.*

WEEK 3
Praying to know...really know Who we belong to!
Ephesians 1:15–23

Have "you" listened to the message of truth, the gospel of your salvation? Have "you" heard that Jesus Christ lived a perfect life under the full weight of the righteous requirements of relationship with a Holy God? Then, He willingly laid down His life, taking on the full wrath of God and payment for sin. He died on the Cross. He was buried. God, the Father, looked at His payment and agreed with Jesus' final words, "IT IS FINISHED!" And Jesus rose from the dead!

Have "you" not only heard, but also believed and trusted in His finished work on the Cross, for you? If so, "you" have been brought from out of relationship with God to "in Him", and sealed with the same Spirit that raised Jesus from the dead…"you" are now *your individual part* of the "we" of God's very own possession! Can I hear an "Amen"!?

We have so much "in Christ." All of us, in Him. We are rich and wealthy beyond anything we can imagine. Paul moves on to a prayer for the saints. This is one of my favorite prayers in all of the New Testament! Let's take a careful look at what he prays and think through the *why*. After his prayer, Paul tells us exactly who Christ is. Be ready to be blown away by Him. This is who we belong to. What can't He do? What does He want to do? Let's see. Make sure to open in prayer.

Week 3—Day 1

Please reread Ephesians 1:1–2:10 to get into the context and see Paul's flow of thought. Remember what God has done through Christ and what that result is for you and me in Him. Take just a minute and thank God for one of His many benefits "in Christ."

Paul reflects on all that God has done (1:15, "for this reason . . ."). Think through for a minute why Paul would insert a prayer here. For what reason can you think of?

He was reflecting on what God has done (vv. 3–14), not just for the saints at Ephesus but also for him. It caused him to thank God and pray. In verses 15–16, what is a practical thing you and I can learn about prayer?

Paul is telling them what he prays, what he wants to see God do, and he writes the result of that answered prayer.

Slowly read 1:16–19. Look over these verses; mull them over. These verses are challenging. In this passage we see some real priorities. When Jesus prays, I take notice; when an apostle prays, I think we should take notice too. What is Paul asking God to do in the lives of these believers and why? Remember whom this book is written to: the average everyday believers/saints, not just the special ones or the real spiritual ones, not even just leadership, but the ordinary ones like you and me. I count three things he asks God to do. Notice that the third thing that he asks has three results.

Let's break it down. What three things does Paul ask God to do/give (vv. 17–19)?

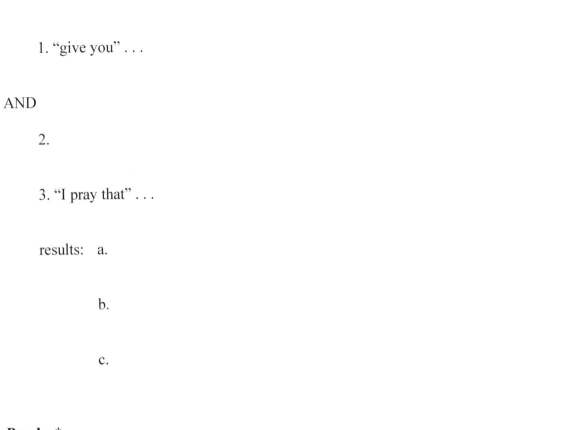

1. "give you" . . .

AND

2.

3. "I pray that" . . .

results: a.

b.

c.

Ponder*
Think about why. Why these three things? Why not, "Lord, let them have happy lives"? Or "Lord, let them grow to be really big and strong in their Christianity." Why?

Look up these words.

v. 17   wisdom (Strong's #4678)

v. 17   revelation (#602)

v. 17   knowledge (#1922)

v. 18   heart (#1271)

v. 18   enlightened (#5461)

After looking at these words, rephrase Paul's petitions in your own words from verses 17–18a. What does he ask God to do for all of these believers? This is some powerful stuff! Tomorrow we will look at the results of this.

Week 3—Day 2

Review the prayer. Which one of these things would you like someone to pray for you? (Just so you know, someone is praying these three things for you.) Stop right now and pray these three things for some believer whom you know. Ask the Holy Spirit to show you whom to pray for.

How would our lives be different as a result of the "eyes of our heart/understanding being enlightened"?

Paul writes the result of enlightened hearts: "so that" what will happen? Fill in the rest of the phrase from verse 18.

    1. you will know . . .

    2. what are . . .

3. what is . . .

Now look up these words:

v. 18   hope (Strong's #1680)

v. 18   calling (#2821)

v. 18   riches (#4149)

v. 18   glory (#1391)

v. 19   exceeding (#5235)

v. 19   power (#1411)

Now rephrase the results from verses 18–19. In your own words, think about what that would look like in a believer's life.

1.

2.

3.

Ask the Holy Spirit right now what He wants to teach you this week. He wants to open your spiritual eyes so that you will *know* who you are in Christ and all that you have.

Week 3—Day 3

If you haven't noticed, there is a lot of *knowing* going on. Is "knowing stuff" an important part of your everyday life?

What would you really like to know? Examples: hobbies, education, yourself, relationships, "how-to" stuff, etc.

Think about it. What does it take to really know any of these things?

That may seem like a dumb question, but it's appropriate. The first thing that comes to my mind is that it takes knowing someone whom I can learn from; then, of course, it takes time, effort, and energy. I'm exhausted thinking about all that it takes to know something. I barely have enough time and energy to brush my teeth at night. What do you think? What kind of power is available to you and me in our walks of life? Is it just enough to fit on the end of a toothbrush? I'll be honest. Sometimes that's exactly how I *feel*—like I'm barely hanging on to the Lord, and that He's giving out just barely enough, certainly not any kind of real abundance. Is that the truth? NO!

Then I have to STOP. Stop thinking that way; stop feeling that way; and stop believing that way. Not just stop but REMEMBER and REPLACE. I have to remember what God's Word says and believe by faith that those words are mine. I need to *know* them.

Look at these references and see what we have now and in the future (not stuff we "maybe" have but for sure have). These are ours "in Christ." They are for every believer!

Romans 8:11

Romans 8:33–39

2 Corinthians 5:21

Colossians 1:27

1 Thessalonians 5:23

Jude 24–25

All of these results do take time, effort, and energy, but whose timetable, effort, and energy? I think Paul is one step ahead of us. Read the rest of verses 19–23.

Week 3—Day 4

Please reread Ephesians 1:1–23 again. What are the "these" in verse 19? Connect the thoughts of the prayer.

Look up the word *accordance* (Strong's #2596). Accordance is the "how." How are all of these things going to be accomplished? How is God going to do all of these things?—answer these prayers to give the spirit of wisdom and revelation and open the eyes of the heart—by the bringing down of God's mighty power and strength (that would be the power of the Holy Spirit, whom you have been sealed with)! Are you getting excited? What did the strength of His might do in verses 20–23? What does that mean for you and me?

What do you learn about Christ in these verses? What did the strength of His might do? Read carefully and see all that Christ has, and all that God did in verses 20–23.

v. 20   raised Christ from the dead

v. 20

v. 21   far above all rule

v. 21   far above . . .

v. 21

v. 21

v. 21

v. 22   put all things in subjection under His feet

v. 22

v. 23   gave Him a body (body of Christ)

v. 23   Christ fills all in all

Which aspect of who Christ is or what He has done hits you the most? Why?

If you are a born again believer, this is whom you belong to! Take a few minutes and sit at His feet and praise His name, His character, who He is—because He is who He says He is and He is worthy!! If you are "in Christ," you belong to HIM.

Week 3—Day 5

Review chapter 1 again. Put it all together and read it with Paul's heart. If you are confused or overwhelmed, just pray and read. Don't get caught up in the homework; get caught up with who our God is, what Christ has done, and who we are now as a result of the finished work of Jesus. Relax into Ephesians 1. Next week we're on to chapter 2.

Spend time with some praise and worship music. Listen to some songs and read the lyrics. Try to focus on songs that sing about who God is or who Christ is and what He has done.

Please don't get me wrong. It's important to know and understand what He has done *for you,* but to truly understand that, you have to know and understand HIM. Sit at His feet and worship Him for WHO HE IS.

WEEK 4
Out ———→ IN = Masterpiece
Ephesians 2:1–10

Last week in your homework, you looked at Paul's prayer for the believers and how all of that is going to be accomplished—in Christ—by His power and authority. Then we got a picture of who Jesus is, what He really has, which is all authority and dominion. ALL!

Also last week, I had you spend some time "at His feet," praising Him for who He is. One of the purposes of worship is not only to see who He is but also to see who we are in the light of Him. To really understand and apply what is ours "in Christ," we have to see who we are or who we were *outside* of Him. The verses we are looking at this week are so powerful, and I can tell you that they have reshaped my view of God's redemptive work in a powerful way.

Let the Holy Spirit show you, teach you, and shape your perspective of mankind. Despite popular belief, there are only two camps: lost and found, saved and unsaved, "in Christ" and outside of Christ. Pray over each day's work and allow it to be a sober time and also a time of rejoicing. I'm praying for you. You are so loved. These verses hold the key to the book. You were born in this day and age for His purposes. Your life and your role matters. It is part of the masterpiece. Make sure to open each time of study with prayer!

Week 4—**Day 1**

You are going to make a long list comparing two things: who I am "in Christ" and who I was outside of Christ. Notice the past tense (was). Here is an important truth: you can only be one or the other—either "in Christ" or outside of Christ. No one is "sort of" in Christ, or only partly outside of Christ. That is not to say we don't look and act like we're outside of Christ, but it is a scriptural impossibility. From an eternal perspective, from God's perspective, we are either "in Christ" or outside of Christ. Do you see the importance of understanding the truth of the gospel? Everything changes in our position—how we are viewed if we are "in Christ."

Review your list from Week 2—Day 3, and then reread chapter 1. Write a list of truths about our position "in Christ," what we have "in Christ," and who we are "in Christ." We are adding to our list of what we learn in chapter 2.

Who I am in Christ

Chapter 1

2:1–10

v. 5

v. 6

v. 6

v. 10

Add to the list from these references. What are you considered? Read these verses and consider what they say about how you are viewed "in Christ" or what you have "in Christ."

Romans 5:1–2, 5, 9–10

Colossians 1:13–14

Ponder*

What do you think? Do you have a lot or just a smidge—hardly enough to get by? I didn't ask how much you feel you have, or how much do you use of what you have. I asked are you seeing how much you *have* in your position of being "in Christ"? The first step to living as we truly *are* is seeing and understanding what you do have as a daughter of the King. You know what else has a huge impact? It is seeing what we *were* outside of Christ. Let me tell you, this is huge. This wasn't just a few of us; this was all of us!

Week 4—Day 2

Today we are going to look at the opposite: who we *were* outside of Christ. This is a simple list but a very important one. I can't emphasize enough how much this has helped me to understand the need I have for what Christ did! This is who I was, but it is no longer who I am!!

Who I was outside of Christ (we are putting together one big list)

Ephesians 2:1–10
1.

2.

3.

4.

5.

6.

7.

Romans 5:6–10
1.

2
.
3.

4.

Colossians 1:13
1.

Colossians 1:21
1.

2.

3.

Now put together the context of these lists. Please look at Romans 5:1–11; Colossians 1:9–22; and Ephesians 2:1–10. Yes, you have already made your lists from these texts, but now I want you to "pull the strings" together—in the concepts and ideas of "in Christ" and outside of Christ. These three texts are doing just that—comparing life outside of Christ and life "in Christ." It is HUGE! Jot down any thoughts or insights.

Week 4—Day 3

Be honest with yourself. Have you really ever considered yourself as an enemy with God? A child of wrath?

Who is in charge of the dominion of darkness? Guess.

Now take a look at these references and see what you learn about Satan. Who is he and what is he called?

John 8:44

John 12:31

1 John 5:19

Read about our problem with sin. What is its result? Who is excluded? Is anyone?

Romans 3:23

These verses speak in the same tense as Ephesians, to those "in Christ." What were we?

Romans 6:17–18

Ponder*

Please end this time considering this truth. We are born in our sin, dead, at war with God—simply because of our position outside of Christ. Sinful. This is big, my sisters, really big. What does this do to the "playing ground" in regard to other people?

Week 4—Day 4

Read 2:1–10. List and consider. What do you learn about God? Look for every reference to Him and record what you learn.

Marking words with symbols (such as a circle) so that they stand out, help us to learn about particular words or phrases. This is very helpful (believe it or not), so we are going to mark a couple of more things.

Reread 2:1–10. Circle every time that you see "in Christ Jesus."

Now what do you learn about being "in Christ"?

What do you learn about where we are positionally now "in Christ" (v. 6)?

When? What kind of time line is God on (v. 7)?

For what purpose and why are we in Christ Jesus (v. 10)?

Finally, according to the text, how would you say that we are to do these "good works" and "walk in them" (v. 10)?

Read over Ephesians 1–2:10 again. Circle the word *grace*.

Look up the word *grace* (Strong's #5485) and write out the definition.

How does grace work? Think of what you have learned. What do we actually deserve based on who we are (were)?

Write down exactly what you learn from each reference to grace in the book of Ephesians so far. Such as, whose is it and who gets it? Where is it from? What does it do or show? And how much of it is shown? Etc.

1:2

1:6

1:7

2:5

2:7

2:8

Week 4—Day 5

Let's see what we learn about grace from some other references. Look at the context and record what you learn. What does grace do? What does it "look" like?

John 1:14–17

Romans 5:1–2

1 Corinthians 15:9–10

Galatians 2:20–21

Hebrews 4:14–16

Let's put it all together. What is Paul's point? Why the talk of grace and who we were outside of Christ? Who needs this grace? For how long? Just to be saved or to walk as well?

Think on this for a minute. If we receive the Holy Spirit upon salvation when we, by faith, trust in Christ Jesus' finished work, then can we "walk" and do "good works" outside of this same grace and faith? Do we try?

Read these verses. Think on their truths and record what you learn about God.

Isaiah 42:8

Isaiah 48:11

Isaiah 61:10

Isaiah 63:5

Ponder*

Who is going to get the glory? Will He share it with anyone? If He won't share His glory for saving us, how can He share His glory for sanctifying us? Look up the word *sanctify* (Strong's #37) and write down its meaning and then answer the questions.

Which is easier for you to focus on: doing things for the Lord? Or being who He has made you to be in Christ? Why?

Is grace a difficult concept for you to accept or not? Is it easy for you to give or not?

It is all about Him. All of it—from the saving to the sanctifying to the day we see Him face-to-face and are changed permanently forever. Can He do it? Can we? Oh, I've tried but it hasn't gone very well. Quite ugly, in fact, and even on my best day when I've tried hard to "do the works," I get the glory. That, my sister, is *not* what He has in mind. That is an attempt to share His glory and He won't share it with anyone.

This walk is a lot less about the *doing* and a lot more about the *being*. If we start being who we are in Christ with the power of His sealed deposit, we will walk by grace and by faith. We will be pleasing Him, not perfectly, hence the grace, but nonetheless pleasing Him—Hebrews 11:6.

WEEK 5
Ripples, Threads and Blocks in the Big Picture
Ephesians 2:11–22

There is a really big picture here—a really big plan from a really big God. The book of Ephesians is six chapters long, with the first three chapters being primarily doctrine (foundational truth). Catch this, if you look for the first instructive command (something he tells them to do), you won't find it until chapter 4, verse 1. I find that interesting. There has to be a reason for this.

If you're anything like me, my natural tendency is to approach things with the attitude of "Here's the plan, this is what needs to be done, tell me what to do, and let's go!" Instead of this strategy, it seems Paul is saying, "Let's slow down, let's get you grounded about who you are 'in Christ,' and let's see God's big picture first, BEFORE I ask you to *do* anything." Novel idea!

Week 5—**Day 1**

With that said, before we get into the "good works" of the "walk" from 2:10, let's get the horse before the cart. Ephesians 1–2:10 is basic, solid truth. As we move on, we are going to take a big-picture look at God's big plan, the church (Christ's body). Review 1:22–23.

Think with me for a minute. When we read 2:8–10, we generally think of our individual salvation and walk—how we have works to do and a walk to walk, right? Of course it is talking about our individual salvation, but is there more?

Consider this: a pool with ripples. A pebble is thrown into the water, it strikes the water, and the ripples start to form. The center ripple is your life and personal walk, and another ripple is your spiritual walk, which ripples to your family, and that ripples to your walk in your church family, which then ripples to your walk in the global/universal church, which ripples out to become the part or role that you play historically in this time and place in history.

This is very conceptual and may sound strange, but from how Paul lays out this amazing book, there seems to be a "ripple effect." In 2:8–10, God has a plan for works and walks on all of those levels. You are part of that. Your part/role matters to the whole. They are interconnected. In other words, our personal walk does not just affect us. We affect each other.

Ponder*
Don't you think we would walk a lot more confidently, boldly, and intentionally if we caught a glimpse of the big-picture plan? Your walk matters to more than just you, your family's, and friends' purposes. Before Paul addresses believers' individual walks (what they are to do), he lays this foundation. He wants them to know that they are a part of a big plan. Don't we all, at the heart of things, want to be a part of something that really matters?

Well, God's plan actually accomplishes all of these things. It's a done deal, because Christ defeated sin and death. We are now a part of the biggest plan and purpose of all time. Paul wanted them and us to understand that we have a role to play, both individually and corporately as a part of the body of Christ.

Read and see the plan unfold. It starts with a new covenant and a better way—in fact, the only way. Unity is now available and that unity is found in Christ's atoning work alone. You are part of a really big plan that will change everything. Please start with prayer.

Read 2:11–22. If you are not familiar with the old covenant/Old Testament, this may seem a little strange, but don't worry; we'll look at it next week. It is totally exciting. Unless you have Jewish blood flowing in your veins, you are a Gentile and so am I. Not only are we Gentiles but we are also women, so from an Old Testament cultural standpoint, we are less than dogs. Doesn't that just sound lovely! Jesus changed all of that!

Week 5—Day 2

First of all, we are going to look at the position of the Gentiles, as a people group. Again, the better we understand what we *didn't have* as Gentiles, the more we appreciate what we *do have* as believers in Christ! Under the economy of the law, there were clear distinctions between Jew and Gentile.

Ponder*
Think through the position of the Gentiles: who they were/how they were considered. What were these Gentiles told to remember? Before they were "in Christ," what were they?

We are the "uncircumcision." What were we considered in verse 12?
    1.

    2.

    3.

    4.

    5.

v. 13   Compare what we were and what we are now "in Christ."

v. 14   What did the dividing wall do? Separated what two groups?

v. 19   We, as Gentiles, are no longer what?
    1.

    2.

The church at Ephesus had a lot of Gentiles but also a good number of Jews. Look for the word *one* in verses 11–22 and circle it. What do you learn?

What do you think is Paul's point about *how* this entire (one body) thing happened?

From God's standpoint, is the new covenant now an issue of being Jewish or being Gentile? Or is it an issue of being "in Christ"? Support your thoughts from the text.

What does this one body (because of what Jesus did) do to the "playing ground" of people, no matter where they come from or where they have been?

Week 5—Day 3

Last week we established that outside of Christ we are at war; in fact, we are enemies with God. In these verses (2:11–22), *who* exactly is Paul talking about? Who was at war with God? Think in terms of covenant.

There are a lot of problems for the Jew and the Gentile. Review. Even under the law, *who* has a problem with sin? Just the Gentiles (Rom. 3:23)?

Is the picture coming together? ALL of mankind, Jew and Gentile alike, were at war and separated from God because of sin. Paul states what Jesus did and how in 2:13–17. What is Jesus called? What did He do?

Slowly read and mark the word *peace.* Make a list of all that you learn about peace. Now do a word study on *peace* (Strong's #1515). What do you learn?

Now read Colossians 1:19–20. Any additional insights?

Read John 14:27–31. This is the Upper Room Discourse right before Jesus is going to Calvary to die. What kind of peace was He talking about, because everything in their world was going to be in complete chaos soon?

Week 5—Days 4 and 5

Mark the word *enmity*. What do you think enmity means? What do you learn about enmity from the two places that it is used? Read it carefully (2:15–16).

Look at these references for additional insight.

Matthew 5:17

Galatians 3:22–25   What is the tutor or teacher?

Don't worry if it's not quite clear yet; it will be! This week the homework is rather conceptual, but we'll pull those loose ends together.

Finally, what are the results of Christ's death, burial, resurrection, and ascension and the coming of the Holy Spirit? The next covenant is now established and in place. Read 2:18–22. Make a list of the results: what we have "through Him."

v. 18   we have access in one Spirit to the Father

v. 19   (remember, we are no longer strangers and aliens), but

v. 19

v. 22

Here's the picture. Write down who is represented in each part of this picture according to 2:20–22. Who is the cornerstone? The foundation? The building? Including who?

Building

Foundation

Cornerstone

Finally, read 1 Peter 2:4–10 and write down any additional thoughts. What are believers called in verse 5? Please just let the beauty of what you belong to sit upon your heart.

Ponder*

Where do you fit? Do you see your part? You have good works to do and a walk to walk in your
> personal life,
> family life,
> church life,
> the life of the church globally, and
> the life of the church historically.

If you are "in Christ," you are part of a big picture and plan. You are part of something that has eternal weight. You are part of something that displays the glory of the God of the universe.

The "playing ground" is level before the Cross, we are all born "out"…no matter what that "out" looked like. I was a good religious girl in my "out-ness", and I looked down on those girls who where "bad", but I was still "out". The wall that separated us was the wall of the law…I thought I was pretty good and they were pretty bad. Jesus broke down that wall, by fulfilling the law for me (the "good girl") and for the "bad girl." Because we both needed peace with God! Jesus is our peace. The ground is just as "level" after we come to Christ for our salvation. In is in. And now, we have been brought "in" to be our part of His Body/Building/Bride/Masterpiece!

Have you ever asked yourself, "What is God's will for my life?" God has a plan and you strategically fit into it. Your place and your role is not an accident, if you catch a glimpse of the big picture of His plan, His will for your life. That takes on a whole different perspective looking at it through His eyes. You are a living stone; you fit. You have been and are being fitted together into a holy temple in the Lord. Think on it, my sister. Pray about it; your part matters!

WEEK 6
Mystery Unveiled...You Fit!
Ephesians 3:1–13

Paul is absolutely convinced that the new covenant is established, and it ushers in one body with Christ as the head—Jew and Gentile alike. All enter one way, by God's grace and through faith because of the finished work of Jesus. This week we'll consider a couple of different angles. To start off, make sure that you are in prayer, asking the Spirit to teach you and enlighten the eyes of your understanding—specifically about His body, the church, of which you and I are a part. Amazingly, our part is as Gentile women, welcomed, loved, and even heiresses.

Week 6—**Day 1**

Read Ephesians 2:19–3:13.

Ponder*
Let's look at this from Paul's perspective. How did Paul view or look at his calling as minister of the gospel to the Gentiles? How did he see his walk and good works that God called him to do: as a blessing or just a job? Did he get the big picture/ripple effect? What did it cost him? Was it easy and filled with fun?

Look at 3:1–13 and see what you glean about his perspective of his calling. What does he call it? Look for words or phrases that he uses in reference to his work. He is in prison as he writes this. Write down your thoughts.

Look for how he viewed his walk/work in a few other places. Please record his perspective.

Acts 9:15–16   What God told Ananias before Paul's sight was returned

Acts 26:12–20 Paul's personal account to King Agrippa

2 Corinthians 11:24–30 Paul describes some ministry experiences

Paul sits in prison because of the gospel of Jesus Christ. He is writing to a primarily Gentile church, which he spent two years building into.

Ponder*
What does he want them to understand? Is he really concerned about what they think of him? How does he view what he is currently going through? Does he sound resentful? How important is it that he operate from the same basis of truth that he is speaking to them about (all being part/with a role/walk/of the body)?

Week 6—Day 2

Today, we'll break it down and see more of Paul's perspective from several other passages. What did Paul call himself or say he was going through in the text of Ephesians 3:1–13?

v. 1

v. 7

v. 8

v. 13

What exactly does he say is his tribulation in verse 13?

Think about that. Let that sit upon your heart. How could he view his trouble/trial for their glory? We're going to "camp" in another place for a few minutes. Read 2 Corinthians 1:3–7 and answer these questions.

What is one of the reasons given for suffering in verse 5?

Look for the word *comfort* in 2 Corinthians 1:3–7. What do you learn?

How would you say Paul viewed his suffering: with his eyes on himself or his eyes on the big picture?

Ponder*
Why did Paul say he suffered? By implication, why do we suffer sometimes? Who is it an opportunity to point to? How does that happen? Can that even begin to happen if we don't know and trust God's character and plan?

Take a look at another place where we see Paul's heart for the Lord and ministry but also a call to all believers about what the love of Christ does in us! This is a "look-up" call to a bigger picture—a call to see that our walk matters and affects others.
Read 2 Corinthians 5:14–6:1 and answer these questions.

In verses 14–16, what controls Paul and why? How much has the "love of Christ" changed him?

He is "spending" himself out on to others for the sake of Christ. How does Paul view all believers? What are they called? Look at verses 16–17. See Galatians 3:28 too. Is there anyone who is not "worth his time"?

In 2 Corinthians 5:18, 20, what does Paul say has been given to him (as well as all believers)?

In 2 Corinthians 5:21 and 6:1, what did Christ do? Why? Any ideas of how we could we "receive the grace of God in vain"?

See his heart, hear his plea, and see the ramifications of the finished work of Jesus. See the call to a life, a walk that does not receive the grace of God in vain. Paul doesn't just teach; he leads by example. This concept is foundational to the book of Ephesians. He is laying a doctrinal foundation of truth (chapters 1–3) before he asks them to "do" anything. He is also leading by example and it is not easy, but it is for the body. In reality, it is for Christ.

Ponder*
How does Paul want his readers to view themselves? This was also a predominately Gentile audience in Corinth. What kind of example was he setting and why? What compelled him?

Week 6—Day 3

The second angle that we want to see in 3:1–13 is from the Jew/Gentile perspective. We can't begin to understand our part if we don't get the big picture of how BIG of a deal it is that we are one body, which includes Gentiles now at peace with God by faith through the atoning work of Christ. That was a mystery.

Reread 3:1–13. As a result of the new covenant, what do Gentiles now have?

v. 6

    1. fellow

    2. fellow

    3. fellow

What does the word *fellow* make you think of in this context? Do you see unity and equality? Or less-than status?

v. 8

As believers in Jesus, as Gentile believers, this is what we have. What do you think of when you hear the word *unfathomable*?

The church age has started and the body of Christ is being formed, a Jew/Gentile body, His bride. Why? What can be made known about God's character in verse 10?

Where and how is "God's manifold wisdom" being shown?

vv. 8–10

How long has this "mystery" (vv. 3–4) been the plan? The answer is in verse 11. Look up the word *mystery* (Strong's #3466) and write about what you learn.

I have tears in my eyes as I type. My sisters, this is so big; this is so God. This is so important to you and me 2000 years later. We are part of a huge story, God's story. This is His love, poured out from before the foundation of the world (1 Peter 1:18–20).

He wants relationship with you, not a distant vague relationship. He wants personal, growing, breathing intimate relationship with you. If you are "in Christ," you are part of the mystery of His body. You fit; you have a part. You are your part of displaying the manifold wisdom of God. WOW!

Week 6—Day 4

Check out these references and look at what you see about God's plan. Sin entered the picture in Genesis 3 and everything for everyone changed. Relationship with God was not possible, but He was making a way: Jesus, who is the way to have relationship with God, not only for the Jew but also for the Gentile.

These next verses were spoken to Abram (later renamed Abraham), who is the physical "father" of Israel. Who is Abraham's line going to affect according to the Scripture?

Genesis 12:1–3 (Jesus is a physical Jew)

Think it through. How are all the nations of the earth going to be blessed through Abraham?

Now read Galatians 3:26–29 and connect the thoughts.

Here is one more place to see the bigger picture. Jesus is speaking to His disciples and the Jews in a metaphor about sheep. Who else is spoken of here and in which verse? Who would the "other" sheep be referring to?

John 10:14–16

Last, read the following reference and see what you learn not only about the Gentiles but also about God's promises to Israel. Paul is writing to the church at Rome, which has big problems between the Jews and Gentiles. Each feels that they are better than the other. God's plan includes both Jew and Gentile.

What do you learn about God's plan?

Romans 11:25–32

He knows that we can't understand it all. Look at how he concludes the thoughts and we'll conclude ours for today here too!

Romans 11:33–36

Week 6—Day 5

Reread Ephesians 1:19b–3:13 and ponder their importance. Pray about why you think this teaching about the church, the Body/Bride/Building/Masterpiece is here. Why is it so important to be placed here before the practical "to-do" stuff? This area is really exciting; please don't be frustrated if you don't get it all or if you don't see its importance. Just sit with the text and then write down any additional insights.

Keep studying, keep seeking, and keep asking Him to show Himself. He is working out great things in you, in His body, and in this world. His plan is not only big but also very good. Re-read Ephesians 2:8-10 again, does the text say that we are His workmanship(s) plural? Or His workmanship singular? Why does that matter? Oh…it matters a lot. You and I are strategically placed in this time and place of history- as part of the manifold wisdom of God- as our individual part of the masterpiece…the same masterpiece of Ephesians 2:10. It's not a mystery anymore…in Christ, you fit!

WEEK 7
Another Prayer to Grow...Deep, Long, High and Wide
Ephesians 3:14–21

This is the last week of "laying the foundation." Paul has spent three chapters (half of the book) laying a solid foundation—a foundation of what God has done through Christ, who we are "in Christ," who and where Jesus is, who we were outside of Christ and how we got into right relationship by grace and faith, building on the truth that there are good works to do and a walk to walk, a body/church to be a part of, a role for each believer to play. Now we will study the closing thoughts of that foundation. I LOVE this!!

Week 7—Day 1

Let's take one more glance and consider 3:13. Paul asks them to not lose heart because of his tribulations for their sake. Look up the phrase *lose heart* (Strong's #1573). Do you think Paul was ever tempted or given a reason to lose heart in his circumstances? Read these references and record what he went through.

Ephesians 6:19–20

2 Corinthians 7:5–6

Paul wasn't a "super Christian" beyond emotions and circumstances BUT he did know how to not lose heart and applied it regularly.

Read 2 Corinthians 4:7–10, 16–18 and answer these questions.

v. 7   What is the "treasure"? What is the "earthen vessel"?

45

Where is the focus? On them or on God? Even though their circumstances are difficult, list the contrasts.

vv. 8–9

    1.   BUT

    2.   BUT

    3.   BUT

    4.   BUT

Look at verse 10. What is the reason *why* they do this?

Read verses 16–18. How do they not lose heart?

Ponder *
Paul had to run the risk of becoming discouraged, but Ephesians 3:13 states for the church at Ephesus not to lose heart. Why? If they lost heart at what Paul went through, how would that affect them? This was not a onetime and I'll never get discouraged and out of focus again. It is a constant fixing, remembering, and refocusing—getting the eyes on the big picture!

Can you imagine how overwhelming Paul's life must have been at times? Think about how overwhelmed you feel sometimes. Honestly, don't you even feel a little overwhelmed by what we are learning? What a huge plan and *I* have an important part to play. You have got to be kidding! If I'm not careful, I might start saying, "What if I don't do my part right?" Or you could say, "What if I do a poor job?" Or "What if I miss what God wants me to do?" "What if I misunderstand him?" AHHH!

Fears within, conflict without! We could be tempted to say, "I don't have enough in me to fail at one more thing; life is too hard, so I just won't try." Can you relate to that thinking? Ladies, with more knowledge comes more responsibility. Feeling overwhelmed yet?

Well, I believe that as the apostle Paul penned this letter, he might have felt the same thing. As he encouraged them not to lose heart, he was also reminding himself not to lose heart. Just as he opened the letter with the truth of who God is and what He has done through Christ, he closes this doctrinal section (chapters 1–3) with a benediction, a wrapping up of thought and focus and he bends his knees and prays.

Oh, ladies, we see a huge key to life "in Christ" and a life walking in the Spirit. Paul focuses on Christ and focuses all his readers on the *how* of things. How is all of this going to be accomplished? By you being overwhelmed and trying hard to work, walk, and play your part? No way. The key to accomplishing anything of eternal value is *Jesus Christ Himself*, His love, and His life-giving Spirit.

Read these beautiful words (3:14–21) and think through these questions.

"For this reason"—for what reason does Paul bend his knees and pray? Why does Paul feel like it's time to pray?

What exactly does Paul ask God to do in verse 16?

Look up these words.

v. 16   strengthen (Strong's #2901)

v. 16   power (#1411)

Can you rephrase what Paul asks God to do?

The power of the Holy Spirit is an amazing thing. What do we learn about the Holy Spirit in these verses?

John 16:7–14

Romans 8:1–4

Romans 8:11

Ponder*
Any thoughts on why strength and power? Does Paul ask God to make it easy for them? To make their walks and lives pretty and painless? Where does he ask God to strengthen them?

Week 7—Day 3

Read 3:14–21 again. He asks for them to be "strengthened with power through His Spirit in the inner man." Why? So that what will happen in their lives (vv. 17–19)?

1.

2.

3.

4.

5.

Now look up these words.

v. 17   dwell (Strong's #2730)

v. 17   grounded (#2311)

v. 18   comprehend (#2638)

v. 19   know (#1097)

v. 19   filled (#4137)

How is it going? Are you currently being strengthened with power by His Spirit? Not just a onetime strengthening but a daily strengthening? What does that look like for you? What does the Bible say that looks like? Let's look at a couple of Scriptures.

John 14:15–19

Galatians 5:16–26

Do you realize that Paul prayed this for *you* specifically? The text says so. Look for it and mark it. How can you support from the text that this prayer is for our generation?

Ponder*
This is powerful, really powerful. What if God answered this in your life daily? Would that be wonderful and life changing, before you even DID a thing? Are you seeing the importance of this prayer?

If you are physically able, I would like to encourage you to get on your knees right now and pray this prayer for yourself, for a believing friend, and for our class.

Week 7—Day 4

We will break this down together, but take some time and consider what Paul is asking and what it will do in the lives of the believers. Why would his focus be there? Why ask God to do this? Now go back to his prayer in Ephesians 1:17–19.

Let's make another list to compare.

What does Paul pray in 1:17–19?

      1.

      2.

      3.

so that it produces

      1.

      2.

      3.

Ephesians 3:14–21?

Paul prays for

      1.

so that it produces

      1.

      2.

3.

4.

5.

Let this sink in. What do our prayers so often look like? What do we ask God to do? Or what do we ask God for? Be honest with yourself.

Read verses 20–21. These are fantastic verses. Answer the following questions.

Who is the "Him"?

How is He going to do this?

What/who is the power that works within us?

Who is going to get the glory?

When will His glory and His church end?

Please take a look at these other great benedictions and see where they all focus. Absolutely, we have something to do, but can any of it be done without Him and without the power of His Spirit? Read the following.

Romans 11:33–36

1 Timothy 6:15–16

Hebrews 13:20–21

Once again, think through the various reasons Paul would conclude the doctrinal part of the book this way before the instructions are given.

Week 7—Day 5

Let's put it all together (chapters 1–3). Reread and see the flow of thought and intention. Allow yourself to be wowed. Yes, this is all about you and your personal relationship with God through Christ, BUT it is also all about you and others—His workmanship, created in Christ Jesus for good works that you may walk in them.

Consider again, as you look over Ephesians 1-3, Paul is not asking them to "do" anything (yet) he is calling them to "be". "Be" who they are in Christ; "be" their part of the masterpiece. Grow deep, high, wide, and long in Christ and His love and power. More times than I can count, I have tried to DO in order to "be"…Paul teaches the reverse. Out of deep "be-ing" comes fruitful "do-ing."

Next week, the *walk* begins, but remember WHOSE walk it is, and in WHOSE power it can only be done. You are loved!!

WEEK 8
Be ⟶ to Do, Now Walk Worthy!
Ephesians 4:1–16

Make sure you start each day with prayer. Pray that the Holy Spirit will open the eyes of your understanding and help you to see and understand the expanse of Christ's love for His bride, which you are a part of if you are "in Christ." This week we are going to see the first instruction to the church at Ephesus—and to us. Take a minute and review. We will have to review the "foundation" because we want to correctly handle the Word and also to remember HOW we are going to do all that is asked. We can't do any of this in our own strength! We need the Spirit's power. We are coming to a bunch of dos and don'ts and if we are not careful, we can become devoted to the list and not the Lord, who made it possible to respond to His call and His work in the first place. So much of this and the Christian life is about perspective and mind-set and remembering WHOSE we are!

Week 8—Day 1

Spend today reviewing these few verses and painting the picture.

Ephesians 1:3, 13, 22
2:8–10, 18–19
3:9–10, 16, 20–21

After spending so much time on the "foundation," write down what has really stuck with you.

What has been most encouraging?

What has been most convicting?

What challenges you the most?

Week 8—Day 2

Now read Ephesians 4:1–3. Let's take a look at this first instruction. Would you call it a command or an instruction or a plea? How would you describe his request? What exactly is the first "thing to do"?

Why does that matter? In your opinion, is Paul being "heavy-handed," a bully, or manipulative in his instruction?

Look up these verses and see if you can see Paul's heart.

v. 1   implore (Strong's #3870)

v. 1   walk (#4043)

v. 1   worthy (#516)

v. 3   unity (#1775)

Use this space to rephrase what Paul is asking these believers to do. Really think it through.

If you were to boil it down to one word, what are these verses calling a believer to be?

Ponder*

"Walk in a manner worthy of the calling with which you have been called." Our walks should be worthy walks. Worthy of who? As a response to who? With our eyes on who? I don't know about you, but too often my eyes are on others and how they treat me and then I respond—sometimes well and at other times not so well. Is that a worthy walk?

Week 8—Day 3

Look at these references and write down what you learn about the calling of our "walks."

Matthew 28:16–20

Romans 12:1–2

Colossians 1:9–12

Colossians 2:6–7

How is this "worthy walk" to be done according to 4:2–3?

With all what?

     1.

     2.

     3.

Honestly, which one is most difficult for you? Which one do you want to be shown to you?

Showing what?

What are we to be diligent in? Why? What is at stake?

We are all running a "faith race." To run a worthy race, where do our eyes need to be? Read Hebrews 12:1–3. What are the instructions in these verses?

Ponder*
Think back over the "foundation" chapters. How have they built up to this first instruction? Who would be excluded from the instruction? Who, if they understood who they really were "in Christ," would not want to do this? Does it seem like a huge request? At a glance, though, do we look like this in the body of Christ?

Week 8—Day 4

What is the big deal about unity? You saw that unity means *oneness* or *unanimity*. But this particular Greek word is from the root word *one* (Strong's #1520). Look up this word and write the definition.

Evidently, unity is a big deal to Paul; he is going to make that very clear. I wonder whom he is modeling?

What does Paul say is *one* in Ephesians 4:4–6?

1.

2.

3.

4.

5.

6.

7.

Why does he say it here? What does he want to remind them of?

Look for the connection between the thoughts—unity yet individuality. Watch how he talks of unity/oneness and then of individuals/parts. What is his point?

To start, read and consider the oneness/parts issue in verses 4–16. Look for it; it sounds like a contradiction of ideas, but is it? What do you learn?

Don't completely skip verses 8–10, but don't get sidetracked on them. We'll hit some highlights later. Jot down your thoughts.

Consider verses 11–16 and make some general observations. Then make two lists.

What are the body/parts is/are to look like in verses 12–13, 15–16?

And

What are the body/parts not to look like in verse 14?

Look up these words for more insight.

v. 16   supplies (Strong's #2024)

v. 16   proper working (#1753)

Ponder*
Where does your part/walk fit? Does it? Are you part of a church family and do you see that you count (not because they say that you do but because He says that you do)? Are you walking worthy and seeking unity? Convicting? Me too. Are you catching the picture that the health of the body of Christ affects you and is affected by you? What are your thoughts and feelings about this? Just consider.

Week 8—Day 5

I realize this may seem a bit vague or disjointed but hopefully it will come together. Look at these references and look for the importance of unity and how each part is playing their role for oneness.

Right before Jesus was betrayed, He prayed for His disciples and for us. John 17 is His High Priestly Prayer. Read these verses and write down what He prayed for. See if He gives a reason for why He prays this way. What are His thoughts about unity and oneness? Why?

John 17:11, 20–23 (If you have time, read the whole chapter. It is wonderful. Look for what Jesus requests of the Father and for whom.)

Paul addressed another church, Corinth, which was really struggling with unity, jealousy, and a bunch of other junk. Read these verses. Where is the focus? What does he liken their church to? And what is his point about, specifically, spiritual gifts? What happens if we don't view our gifts, walks, and lives as a part of a whole body?

1 Corinthians 12:4–7, 12–27 (Again, if you have time, read chapter 13. It should sound familiar. We like to bring it out for weddings but the context is unity in the midst of the body of Christ!)

If the parts don't work right together, what kind of body is it?

Recap according to Ephesians 4:1–16. Is our personal walk to look like something? What? Does it just affect us?

What does "walking worthy" have to do with unity and oneness and parts working together as a whole?

If it all seems a bit cloudy, this is a great time to talk with another sister. Our "parts" will help each other. Hey, novel idea! Could that be a "God thing"? You are so valuable and your part matters to the whole. It matters for your sake but also for others' sakes. YOU matter. Your life and walk matter. His body needs your part in order to be whole, mature, and healthy.

WEEK 9
Be ⟶ to Do, Now Walk Differently!
Ephesians 4:17–32

This week is when the rubber is really going to meet the road. We are going to see another way how our walks are supposed to look. Our walk is supposed to look different than the worlds. Why? Because we actually *are* different. Our position has changed; we are now "in Christ." We are no longer old, but new. We are no longer dead, but alive. We are no longer slaves, but free. We are no longer out, but in. Our desires, motives, actions, words, attitudes, well…everything is now "on the table" for the Lord to use. Our walk, our lives are now His. Will we corporate, yield and submit?

Week 9—Days 1

Verse 17 says "walk not longer just as the Gentiles also walk." Following verse 17, there is a really big list of do's and don'ts, but before we get all uppity about how different we are in our walks, let's review who we used to be.

Read Ephesians 2:1–7 again. If you are like me, I can get so caught up in the dos and don'ts and the being different that I can tend to isolate myself instead of shining as a light. What did Jesus say in the Sermon on the Mount? Read Matthew 5:13–16. What's the plan? We are to affect the lost and dying world with our very lives. Our walk, our pattern of life, is to look like something for a purpose. How does our walk become the walk it's supposed to be? It has to all be done by His power, in His grace, and by faith. But again, how? Let's get started.

Ephesians 2:10 says, "For we are His workmanship, created in Christ Jesus for good works, which God prepared beforehand so that we would *walk* in them."

> Walk worthy (4:1)
> Walk differently (4:17)

Walk different than what? (Our former way of life)
Read 4:17–19 and think through the former life.

Gentiles (unbelievers) walk

v. 17

v. 18

v. 18

Why are they excluded from the life of God?

Because of

v. 18

v. 18

And the result of that is
(Having become what, and given themselves over to what?)

v. 19

v. 19

v. 19

Titus also gives us a picture of this life outside of Christ—a life you and I were a part of—in fact, everyone was or is. Read Titus 3:3–8. Remember, this is a blanket statement, not just a list of symptoms. This is our condition outside of Christ. This is what we were rescued from! Don't you think that is a great reason to walk differently?

Week 9—Days 2 and 3

Read Ephesians 4:20. Rephrase this verse in your own words.

Ponder*
There is a contrast of lives: the old/former and the new. What are we to do, and how are we to do it? I know I'm supposed to be different but *how*? Do you think walking differently is deliberate or by accident? How difficult is it to live differently?

Read 4:22–24 and look at the *how*. How are we to walk differently?

What do these verses say we are to do? Look for the verbs (action words).

1.

2.

3.

Look up the following.

v. 22   lay aside (Strong's #659)

v. 23   renewed (#365)

v. 24   put on (#1746)

If you can, please look up the verb tenses. It is very interesting.

Now rethink the three "to dos" with these definitions. Restate what "to do."

Ponder*
What do these words imply about a time line in life? Is this just a onetime thing? Does this happen by accident? Is our Christian life/walk and testimony a fifty-yard dash or a marathon race? How would renewing fit into the race?

For additional insight, what exactly is to be laid aside?
Hebrews 12:1–3

What do you think of when you hear the word *renew*? What does renewing look like?
Romans 12:1–3

Look at what we see about the "new self." Read and record.

Colossians 3:1–17

2 Corinthians 5:17, 21

The verb tenses for put off and put one are onetime events…where renewing is a continuous action. When what the old life put off and the new life put one?

Just think through the contrast between the former life and the new life according to these passages (which we've studied on Days 2 and 3). To help you see this and focus your thoughts, answer briefly.

How did you get the new life in Christ?

How are you to live it out?

In whose strength and power?

Are you going to be perfect?

How long is it going to take? See Philippians 1:6.

But, think . . .

Do we have to commit to pursuing this? Is there some responsibility on our part? Again, see Ephesians 4:22–24.

Week 9—Day 4

Let's make a big list. Read Ephesians 4:25–32. List what we are called to do and not do.

DO NOT   DO

Ponder*

Are you seeing an answer to *why* in any of these verses? *Why* walk differently? How does this list of do's and do not's affect unity in the body and relationships with each other? Is walking differently just about us and our personal walk?

Look up the word *grieve* (Strong's #3076). Look for a synonym of the word, because a command of "do not" in connection with the Holy Spirit seems serious to me. What do you learn? What does *grieving* the Holy Spirit look like?

Week 9—Day 5

This section in Ephesians 4 is extremely practical and should seem a bit like "duh" stuff, but is it? Honestly, which one of the do not's do you struggle with the most? Me? Probably, being angry and not sinning. I have both down pretty well—being angry and sinning! I have had some serious anger issues in the past—in the past five minutes! Okay, just kidding ya, kind of!!! Anger has been a real battleground for me.

These are the keys that are helping my life to be transformed—not perfectly but progressively: recognizing that my old self is dead and can bring nothing but death; being renewed in my mind continually by the Spirit with the Word; and "sinking into" my new self, who I am in Christ. I can honestly say that I can look back and see a change. I'm not as angry as I was a year ago and five years ago. Know what I mean? BUT I can't take the credit—the Lord gets it. The Spirit is changing me.

Oh, if I mess up, and I am convicted and I choose NOT to listen to the Spirit, what happens? I grieve the Holy Spirit. I put Him in the corner. Are you seeing how all of these things are connected? Are you catching a glimpse? My prayer is that you are. My sisters, we belong to the One who changes lives. His gospel works. We are called to a walk, one that is worthy and different.

Please look up the following references. Record what you learn. These all deal with some of the same types of issues and how we are to walk differently by the power of the Holy Spirit.

Colossians 3:8–14

2 Thessalonians 3:7–13

James 1:19–22

1 Peter 3:8–9

Hopefully, you are seeing what life "in Christ" looks like. It's worthy because He is worthy and He has made us worthy. It is a calling and it looks different than the world. It's a transformation. Close today by reading Revelation 1:5–6. Priests have a job to do. One of their jobs is to represent God to the people.

Ponder *
Are you being changed? What are you representing to this lost world? What are you representing to the hurt and wounded around you? Are you demonstrating the good news that they can be saved and changed too?

You and I were once lost and wounded. Though it may have looked different for each of us on the outside (because some are really "big" sinners in our estimation)—but lost is lost. We are now found, and it is NOT for the purpose of isolation but for illumination—to be different, to be Jesus! Walk worthy, walk differently….we are all walking, the question is: how?

WEEK 10
Be → to Do, Now Walk in Love and as Children of Light!
Ephesians 5:1–14

We are His workmanship, His finished work, with our own good works to do along with our own walks. The call here is to discipleship, a worthy walk. This walk is different than the worlds and different than our former life. Now it is also a walk in love and a walking as we are—children of Light. That is what we will see this week.

Ephesians 2:10 says, "For we are His workmanship, created in Christ Jesus for good works, which God prepared beforehand so that we would *walk* in them."

Walk worthy (4:1)
Walk differently (4:17)
Walk in love (5:1)
Walk as children of Light (5:8)

How did Jesus say the world would know His disciples? Read John 13:34–35. Pray as you begin each day. May we be rooted and grounded in the fact that HE loved us first.

Week 10—Day 1

Read Ephesians 4:29–5:2. Review the contrast between what "to do" and what "not to do" in these verses.

"Therefore be imitators of God, as beloved children" (5:1).
Look up these words.

v. 1   imitators (Strong's #3402)

v. 2   love (#26)

How is being an "imitator of God" reflected in these verses (4:9–5:2)?

What did Christ do? Read Isaiah 53:5–7.

See part of how it happened with Jesus. Did Jesus give us something to imitate that relates to 4:29–32? Read and reflect on His sacrifice and example. Think through what He did that relates to the following verses.

Matthew 26:47–54

Matthew 26:59–64

Luke 23:33–43

John 19:26–27

Week 10—Day 2

How is Christ's love described in verse 2?

What does 1 John 4:7–11, 19 give as the reason for loving others? Who loved first?

Ponder*
We'll talk about *agape* love this week, but why do you think there is this instruction to *walk in love*? What's love got to do with it? Read the rest of this section (Eph. 5:1–14) and start to think through the connection of a walk in love, our behavior, and walking as children of Light. What is the connection? Is there one?

Who set the example for us by walking the ultimate walk of love? The "love" section in 1 Corinthians 13 (which we may be familiar with) is talking about *agape* love—God's love. It was walked out perfectly in the person of Jesus Christ. Read 1 Corinthians 13 and see what God's love really is—not ours but His. We cannot begin to display it without Him.

More lists!
Love is . . .

Love is not . . .

What does love do in "all things"?

Week 10—Day 3

What is the connection to our behavior? List the dos and don'ts of Ephesians 5:3–7.

DON'T   DO

In verse 7, it says that we are not to be partakers with them. Why?

Review the following verses about what the flesh produces and what Christ has done for us.

Romans 7:19–25

1 Corinthians 6:9–20

Look up the following words.

v. 7   partaker (Strong's #4830)

v. 8   light (#5457)

Read verse 8 carefully. What were we then and what are we now?

Week 10—Day 4

Read Colossians 1:9–13. What are we *now* in regard to Light? How were we rescued? What do you think of when you hear the word *rescue*?

We are no longer of the darkness. Read Acts 26:18 and let it sink in.

Read Ephesians 5:8–14. Circle the word *light* and record what you learn about it. What does it do or produce?

What does light do to darkness? When you walk into a dark room and turn on the light, what happens?

If we are not careful, how could we interpret verse 11? Could it be like a searchlight?

Read the following references that deal with walking in the light. What does light do?

Philippians 2:14–16

1 Peter 2:9–12

What else do you glean from this passage about what our walks look like, in love and as children of Light?

Week 10—Day 5

Now we are going to read and study Galatians 5:13–26. The word for *light* in Ephesians 5:9 is actually a different Greek word than the other lights used in the passage. It is the word for Spirit, the Holy Spirit. Read Galatians 5:13–26 and answer the questions. This passage is talking about walking in the Spirit. Do you see a connection to our Ephesians passage?

Mark your page (if you can) or just start making a list of what you learn about the Spirit in Galatians 5:13–26.

Holy Spirit

Look specifically for verbs (action words) connected with the Spirit.

v. 16

v. 17

v. 18

v. 25

What does the Spirit want to do in the life of every believer? Yes, produce fruit but what else?

How would grieving the Spirit (Eph. 4:30) cause some of the problems in Galatians 5?

What does Galatians 5 teach us about our walk and the Spirit?

You are doing such a great job! I hope and pray that you are being challenged to think—not necessarily getting all the answers but thinking. I hope you see that this walk is a living, breathing relationship with our heavenly Father, Jesus Christ, and the Holy Spirit. These last two weeks have been hitting us in our walks in and around the world. They have hit us directly about our behavior. Thanks for learning with me. We need each other! This walk is designed for walking with one another.

Be encouraged; you play a huge part in a wonderful plan!

WEEK 11
Be → to Do, Now Walk Wisely!
Ephesians 5:15–6:9

We are about to see the last part of the description of our "walk." It is to be a careful walk, in wisdom. Oh, that we may be wise women. King Solomon wrote in Proverbs 1:7, "The fear of the Lord is the beginning of knowledge; fools despise wisdom and instruction." Ladies, we want to be wise women who respect God, not just in word but in deed—in our hearts. Please pray as you do your homework. We'll be looking at a large section of Scripture dealing with the body, the home, and the world.

Remember Ephesians 2:10. "For we are His workmanship, created in Christ Jesus for good works, which God prepared beforehand so that we would *walk* in them."

> Walk worthy (4:1)
> Walk differently (4:17)
> Walk in love (5:1)
> Walk as children of Light (5:8)
> Walk wisely (5:15)

Week 11—Day 1

Please read Ephesians 5:15–21 and answer the following questions.
Look at the instruction "be careful." What does that imply about being able to walk wisely?

What hits you about these verses? Why is making the most of our time a wise thing?

Look up the following words.

v. 15   careful (Strong's #199)

v. 15   wise (#4680)

v. 16   making the most (#1805)

v. 18   filled (#4137)

Now, slow down. What exactly does this careful walk in wisdom look like? Make a list of what is a wise walk and an unwise walk.

Wise walk   Unwise walk

How is the idea of being a watchman (wise) conveyed in these verses?

Week 11—Day 2

Look up these verses and write down what you learn about wisdom and its ramifications.

Proverbs 2:1–10

Proverbs 4:5–13

James 1:5–6

James 3:17–18

What are some results of being filled by the Holy Spirit in 5:19–21?

Look at this parallel passage in Colossians 3:15–16 and see what you learn.

Ponder*
Can we "do" those things without being filled by the Holy Spirit? Is that wise? If we just "do" things, does that mean we really understand what God's will is?

Week 11—Day 3

We are simply going to review the flow of the book. Think about what we know to be true about us and God's will—also, what we know about how all of this is to be accomplished.

Ephesians 1:3

1:13–14

1:22–23

2:4–10

3:8–10

3:14–21

4:1

4:13–17

5:1–2, 8

Finally, read, think through, and write 5:21.

Look up this phrase.

v. 21   be subject (Strong's #5293)

Restate verse 21, keeping in mind the connection to the book.

Now think through the order of things. Who is at the "top"? Who is the head, according to 1:22?

Before you get yourself in a tizzy about the submission issue, what does 5:21 say? Be subject to whom, and how?

Week 11—Day 4

Whenever we start talking about the "S" word (submission), I start to feel a bit claustrophobic. I have to tell myself to breathe in and breathe out. What if submission opens the door to being a doormat? Personally, I'm not a big fan of mud on my back. What does this issue really boil down to?

Faith! Faith in WHOM we are ultimately submitting to. We'll talk more about this but consider what these two passages say about submission in general.

1 Peter 5:5–11

Will it (submitting) always be pretty and easy?

Are our issues unique?

When we practice biblical submission, whom are we really coming under?

Do you see any attitudes connected to submission?

Jot down any comments about the connection of thoughts of anxiety and submission.

Read slowly and consider Philippians 2:1–11. This is a wonderful passage about mutual submission among other things. Does Christ ask us to do anything He didn't do before us? Why did He submit? What was the result?

What does Paul instruct these believers to do?

What did Christ "give up" or what did it cost Him? Why did He do what He did?

Look for any attitudes that Christ displayed. What were they?

Why can we perceive humility/submission as humiliating? In reality, spiritually, is it?

Thanks for hanging in there. We're coming close to the end of our study. Next week we'll start to see what is really at stake. The times are evil (5:16) and it is a war. BUT we are HIS and He is the VICTOR!

Ponder*
Okay, think through this with me for a minute. Paul is addressing all saints within a church at a particular place, and he has addressed how their walks are going to look. Right? Now he is going to shift gears and talk specifically about roles within a family: husbands, wives, children, masters, slaves. Why?

Finally, compare verses 21 and 22. Who is subject to whom? Is that a bad thing?

Week 11—Day 5

Read Ephesians 5:22–6:9. We will see some areas here, such as, in the home, in the body of Christ, and in the world. Can you see the distinction?

Ponder*
Think through what is being talked about and how living life this way would affect a family and a community of believers, even a community of unbelievers. Replace the master/slave thought with an employer/employee thought. How would Christ be represented in our world if we lived this way? How would His body be represented?

Look for the word *love* and circle it. What do you learn about love?

Ponder*
Do you think there is any connection to the concept of love and submission? Think on it—love to whom or from whom and submission to whom? Think about any connections that you might see.

Read 5:22–23. Look carefully, but don't over think it. Slow down and see what Paul is saying. What is the real comparison? We'll talk about it this week. Make several lists. What do you learn about the following?

Husbands/wives

Christ/church

I'd like you to ponder a thought with me, which concept came first? Christ and the Church or marriage between a husband and wife? Did God pattern Christ and the Church (Bride) after

Adam and Eve or vice versa? Which pattern is eternal? Which is temporary, until death do us part? What do you learn?

Now read 6:1–9.

Home life/children

Workplace/slave/master

Finally, read Revelation 19:5–13.
What is being celebrated here? With whom?

Thank you for hanging in there. There is so much in the Word that fits together; there is so much in the book of Ephesians that fits together. Remember that Paul did not sit down and say, "Chapter 1, verse 1, etc." It was all one, big letter—a connected letter, not just random thoughts. You are loved, my sisters. You have been purchased. You are part of a huge plan. You have a place. You are called to works, you are called to a walk, and you are accountable. You have a POWER SOURCE. You are to submit—all in the NAME OF LOVE.

WEEK 12
Now Stand
Ephesians 6:10–13

This week we are looking at a small passage—only four short verses. We are going to see what is at stake here, what we are a part of. We are at war. The question is, with whom? I act like I'm at war with the world sometimes, and usually that looks like I'm at war with people. We're not in that kind of war.

I'll be honest, for me the battle is to stand on what is true about my position in Christ, because it's true. Sometimes I have to stand, sit, cling, or drop in a heap on what is true. My sister, this battle is real. We must know what is true so we can stand, in Him!

Please open with prayer each time you study.

Week 12—Day 1

We are going to look at this from several standpoints this week. We'll look at who our battle is with, where it is, and why it matters. I'm sure some of you are familiar with this passage. Next week we'll look at our battle dress. These are wonderful concluding words, and a concluding, closing focus.

Read Ephesians 6:10–13. First of all, write down all of the commands. What does Paul say to do?

vs. 10–11

v. 13

What does Paul repeat, just to make sure they get it?

How much of the armor is to be put on?

What are the results? What does the armor do in verses 11 and 13?

Who is the battle against? Who is it not against? Any ideas why?

Please take a minute and put all of this into a chart—the same questions but in a different format.

Write each command/instruction.

v. 10

v. 10

v. 11

v. 13

What will the armor do?

v. 11

v. 13

v. 13

v. 13

The battle is against who?

    1.

    2.

    3.

    4.

The battle is not against . . . , then where is the battle?

Think it through. What else is in the heavenly places?

1:3

1:20

2:6

3:10

Is this battle real, even if we can't see it? Think about all that is taking place in the heavenly places. What is God's perspective of the battle? What is His perspective of your personal battle if you are His? What is our perspective about our battles?

Week 12—Day 2

Ladies, do you see it!? If we are His, then the battle/victory is His and ours—IN CHRIST. Please do these word studies. Let this truth really start to formulate!
Look up the following.

v. 10   strong (Strong's #1743)

v. 10   in (#1722)

v. 10   power (#2904)

v. 11   put on (see 4:24, same word; #1746)

v. 11   stand (#2476)

v. 11   schemes (#3180)

v. 13   resist (#436)

v. 13   done (#2716)

Please look at the definitions and rethink the verses (6:10–13).

Ponder*
What is the only guarantee to stand in the battle? Why is that? Why is it so easy to look at people and circumstances as the real battlefield? How can this be a healthy change of perspective to see our lives as a spiritual battle?

Week 12—Day 3

Okay, let's see more about this battle. The battle is not against people; it is a spiritual battle. Describe what you think the battle looks like. Personally, I think it is different for each of us on some level and also much the same.

Look at these references and see what you glean about our battle.

1 Corinthians 10:12–14

James 4:4–8

1 Peter 5:6–9

This is just a glimpse. What is a common denominator that you see on *our* part in these verses and what warning is given?

Ponder*

What are the "schemes of the devil"? What is his goal in the life of a believer? If he can't have your soul, what would he love to do? Is he a real threat?

How big of a deal is pride to God? Did you see that Satan and our pride are directly connected? Has Satan used it before? Check out Genesis 3:1–13 and 1 John 2:15–17. What do you learn about how Satan works on and with our pride?

What is Satan's goal in the life of the believer? If he can't have our soul, what would he love to do? Keep us useless and unfruitful in our walks….keep us immature see 2 Peter 1:2-9.

Week 12—Days 4 and 5

We've spent some time this week looking at the battle and the real enemy. Now, we need to spend the rest of the time looking at what we have! We have strength in the Lord and His might. We have armor (we'll look at that next week). We are able to stand! To stand!

Ponder*

What do you think of when you think of standing—in battle of all things? In order to stand, what is there a lack of and what is there a supply of? Don't forget it says to stand firm. What do you think of when you hear *firm*?

We have His strength and might. How and from where? Review what we learned about God's mighty strength in Ephesians 1:19–23.

What else do you learn about His strength and might from the following references?

Philippians 4:12–13

2 Thessalonians 3:3

Revelation 5:11–13

I'm still pondering the standing firm thing in the midst of the battle. Wow! I'd like you to wrap up this week by looking at the concept of *stand*ing in the New Testament. What are we called to stand in? Stand for? Who is going to make us stand?

Each of the following references has the word *stand* in them. Comment on what you learn about standing.

Romans 5:2

Romans 14:4

Romans 14:10

1 Corinthians 16:13

Philippians 4:1

Jude 24–25

Ephesians 6:13b says, "and having done everything, to stand firm."

We have a walk to walk, my sisters. We are His workmanship. We have good works to do. We have a battle to fight in. If you haven't heard, we win because He won. What do we forget we have? Where are our eyes: on the battle or on Him? What is the full armor? Paul has laid out the foundation. Remember who you are and to WHOM you belong. Remember what is in the heavenly places. Remember to be strong in the Lord and in the strength of HIS might. We'll look at the armor next week. What we have available makes us more than prepared. You are loved, my sister. We are more than conquerors in Christ Jesus.

WEEK 13
The Armor
Ephesians 6:14–18

Last week we saw that we are all in a battle, and "in Christ" we are victorious in that battle. Warren Wiersbe once said that as believers, "We are working from a position of victory; we are not working for victory." I'll be honest; so often that is not how I feel. The reality is, however, we truly are in a position of victory—"in Christ."

All of this makes me pause and wonder what the armor has to do with this victory. Do I take the armor seriously? Paul certainly did, so let's take a look at what this armor is and what it does. Please make sure you are in prayer each time you study. This is a lengthy lesson but straightforward.

Week 13—Day 1

Read Ephesians 6:14–18. What is the armor and how much are we to put on?

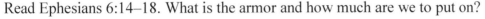

    1.

    2.

    3.

    4.

    5.

    6.

We are going to take a look at the whole armor this week. I'll have you look in various places to see what you glean from God's Word, and I'll also ask you some questions to get you thinking about the nature of the battle and why we need armor. Be encouraged! This will be fun. Feel free to jot down any thoughts or things you have heard about this passage. Remember to think "Roman." Roman? Yes, think it through from a first-century perspective. Rome was a fighting machine, and these people would easily be able to relate to battle and armor from a very different perspective than we do. Let your imagination run a bit.

You are being prayed for consistently. Know that no matter what your battle looks like, God is aware and in control. He has you here for a reason. You are loved and "in Christ"; you're a conqueror (Rom. 8:37).

Week 13—Day 2

Read Isaiah 11:1–5. What is the Lord going to do? Who is being talked about here?

Read Matthew 1:5–6, 16. See the genealogy and how Jesus came to earth to battle for us and won. He is the victor and now we are here—in this time and place, a part of His body—and we are to fight, in His Power, in His strength and might. We are to stand. We are to wear His armor, the armor that He purchased for us. It's God's. Let that sink in and let's take a look at this armor.

Gird your loins with truth (other versions say belt of truth)

Ponder*
First of all, what does a belt do? What would a belt do especially in a culture where men wore robes, and these men were getting to ready to run in battle?

What do we learn about truth? There are a lot of verses but jot down what you learn.

Psalm 119:142, 160

John 1:14, 17

John 8:32, 44

John 14:6

John 16:13

John 17:17

1 Timothy 3:15

Ponder*

How do you think truth plays out in this battle? In a culture that says truth is relative, is it important to know what you believe about truth? Is there absolute truth?

Week 13—Day 3

Put on the breastplate of righteousness

Okay, dumb question. What body part does a breastplate cover?

What do the following references have to do with righteousness? Where is righteousness found? Ponder and think about the context of this. Who has a problem? What is it and who is being talked about?

Isaiah 59:14–17, 20

1 Corinthians 1:30–31

2 Corinthians 5:21

Shod your feet with the preparation of the gospel of peace

Where do our feet take us? How intentional do we need to be in our interaction with other believers and the world? Why the gospel of peace?

Isaiah 52:7

Romans 10:12–15

1 Peter 3:14–16

Week 13—Day 4

Take up the shield of faith

What do you think of when you think of a shield? I think of the gladiator movies and that little round shield thing on their arms. Not so; look up the word *shield* (Strong's #2375). We'll look at some other words together, but you have got to see this!

What is this shield of faith able to do according to this passage (6:16)? How many of the arrows?

Think of the shield. Then think of this: How do we perceive our faith? What is faith?

Let's see what we learn about faith in the following references.

Romans 8:24–25

2 Corinthians 5:6–7

Hebrews 11:1, 6

How does our battle often look? How does the shield of faith work (in the following)?

Romans 10:17

Galatians 2:19–3:2

Take the helmet of salvation

How do the following references deal with the helmet of salvation? What does a helmet protect? How are our minds at war?

Isaiah 59:17

Romans 7:18–25

2 Corinthians 10:3–6

Colossians 3:1–3

Week 13—Day 5

Take the sword of the Spirit

What is the sword? All of this armor so far has been defensive. This is the only offensive weapon given—the only part that fights and does damage!

What do we learn about the Word of God in the following?

Psalm 19:7–13

Romans 15:4

2 Timothy 3:16–17

Hebrews 4:12–13

Ladies, we are in a battle. BUT if we are "in Christ," if we are His, then we are not only secure but also victorious, no matter what things *look like* or *feel like*. The armor is vital though; it protects and prepares us. End with these two passages and just reflect on WHOSE we are and what Christ's work has accomplished—John 10:27–30 and Revelation 12:10–11.

Are you seeing how Jesus is the fulfillment of every piece of armor? As we rest in Him, in our secure position and identity in Him....we stand.

WEEK 14
Love and A Look Back
Ephesians 6:19–24 and Review

This is it, my sisters—our last week in this great book. My prayer is that you have caught a glimpse of who you are "in Christ" and what has been given to you. I pray that you see that you are part of a wonderful huge plan with a role to play and a walk to walk. Our walk reflects the heart of God to a lost world, and we are at war—not with the world but with Satan and his domain. BUT we are victorious because of our position in Christ! Now, we get to work that out into our practical lives, with purpose and with power. HIS POWER!!

Please pray as you finish this week. One final thought on the battle: Was Paul in his own battle? Where was he when he wrote this letter? As you read this closing section, what specifically does he ask them to pray for?

Week 14—Days 1

With all prayer

Review Ephesians 6:10–24. Then read 6:18–19. Think it through. Is prayer part of the armor? What is Paul saying about the importance of prayer? Why?

Review what Paul has already prayed for these believers in Ephesians 1:15–19 and 3:14–21.

How are we to approach this battle that all Christians are in (including you and I)?

What feelings stir in you at the thought of being in a battle?

Boldness is not at the top of my list, so why boldness? Why would he ask for boldness? That is such an amazing thought—boldness in battle. What would give Paul boldness?

Week 14—Days 2 through 5

We will spend the rest of our time in review. Actually, I'm going to have you redo part of your homework from week 1 (just taking another look at the middle of the book between the bookends)! You'll be amazed at what you have learned. Look at it with fresh eyes, enlightened eyes. Take a couple of days and read the entire book of Ephesians (use the text that we gave you) and start thinking/examining Paul's flow of thought.

Write down what you think his main point is. In other words, what is he talking about or what does he seem to emphasize? In each of these segments below, just jot down simple, general thoughts. Pray before you begin, and then let your mind start digging into this great book. Don't over think. We are putting the corner and edge pieces together of the puzzle of Ephesians. (First, bookends, now puzzles!) There are no right or wrong answers, just observations. What does he want them to understand in these segments? Please list a few thoughts.

  Segment 1   1:3–2:10

  Segment 2   2:11–3:13

  Segment 3   3:14–21

  Segment 4   4–6:9

  Segment 5   6:10–24

Think about what you learn about this word and this phrase.

Walk

In the heavenly/in the heavenly places

Write down your thoughts or just think and pray about the following.

1. What do you think of when you hear the word "walk"?

2. Now that you have studied the book, can you think of some examples of what "the walk" Paul is talking about might look like today for you and me?

3. What exactly is in the "heavenly places"?

4. Where are the heavenly places?

Before we end this book, I just want you to review one more thing. Exactly where does he focus the readers at the very end of the letter in verse 24?

Now review Revelation 2:1–4 (which is sixty plus years later). What ended up happening generations after this book was written?

Ponder*
Ladies, how are we doing growing in and understanding the love of Christ? How are we doing passing that love on to others? What are our goals in regard to this? Here we see Paul's goal: 1 Timothy 1:5.

Do you see what eventually happened at the church at Ephesus? They were "doing," they knew truth and stood on it, fought for it, but they forgot to "be" before they "do-ed." They lost their first love; they lost sight of who they were "in Christ." They lost sight of Jesus, the One, the Head, the Life, the Love.

You have so much; you are blessed beyond your wildest dreams. You're an heiress in an eternal kingdom. You are a princess and daughter of the King. You've been graced! You are beautiful and priceless. You are loved. If you have come to Christ in faith and by His grace for the salvation of your sins, by His finished work on the cross, you are "in Christ." You are His workmanship, and you have a walk to walk until you see Him face-to-face. Now, "in Christ," walk by grace and faith!

EPHESIANS

1   Paul, an apostle of Christ Jesus by the will of God, to the saints who are at

Ephesus and who are faithful in Christ Jesus:

2   Grace to you and peace from God our Father and the Lord Jesus Christ.

3   Blessed be the God and Father of our Lord Jesus Christ, who has blessed us

with every spiritual blessing in the heavenly places in Christ,

4   just as He chose us in Him before the foundation of the world, that we would be

holy and blameless before Him. In love

5   He predestined us to adoption as sons through Jesus Christ to Himself,

according to the kind intention of His will,

6   to the praise of the glory of His grace, which He freely bestowed on us in the

Beloved.

7   In Him we have redemption through His blood, the forgiveness of our trespasses,

according to the riches of His grace

8   which He lavished on us. In all wisdom and insight

9   He made known to us the mystery of His will, according to His kind intention

which He purposed in Him

10   with a view to an administration suitable to the fullness of the times, that is, the

summing up of all things in Christ, things in the heavens and things on the earth.

In Him

11   also we have obtained an inheritance, having been predestined according to His

purpose who works all things after the counsel of His will,

12   to the end that we who were the first to hope in Christ would be to the praise of

His glory.

13   In Him, you also, after listening to the message of truth, the gospel of your

salvation—having also believed, you were sealed in Him with the Holy Spirit of

promise,

14   who is given as a pledge of our inheritance, with a view to the redemption of

God's own possession, to the praise of His glory.

15   For this reason I too, having heard of the faith in the Lord Jesus which exists

among you and your love for all the saints,

16   do not cease giving thanks for you, while making mention of you in my prayers;

17   that the God of our Lord Jesus Christ, the Father of glory, may give to you a spirit

of wisdom and of revelation in the knowledge of Him.

18   I pray that the eyes of your heart may be enlightened, so that you will know what

is the hope of His calling, what are the riches of the glory of His inheritance in the

saints,

19   and what is the surpassing greatness of His power toward us who believe.

These are in accordance with the working of the strength of His might

20   which He brought about in Christ, when He raised Him from the dead and seated

Him at His right hand in the heavenly places,

21   far above all rule and authority and power and dominion, and every name that is

named, not only in this age but also in the one to come.

22   And He put all things in subjection under His feet, and gave Him as head over all

things to the church,

23   which is His body, the fullness of Him who fills all in all.

Chapter 2

1   And you were dead in your trespasses and sins,

2   in which you formerly walked according to the course of this world, according to

the prince of the power of the air, of the spirit that is now working in the sons of

disobedience.

3   Among them we too all formerly lived in the lusts of our flesh, indulging the

desires of the flesh and of the mind, and were by nature children of wrath, even

as the rest.

4   But God, being rich in mercy, because of His great love with which He loved us,

5   even when we were dead in our transgressions, made us alive together with

Christ (by grace you have been saved),

6   and raised us up with Him, and seated us with Him in the heavenly places in

Christ Jesus,

7   so that in the ages to come He might show the surpassing riches of His grace in

kindness toward us in Christ Jesus.

8   For by grace you have been saved through faith; and that not of yourselves, it is

the gift of God;

9   not as a result of works, so that not one may boast.

10 For we are His workmanship, created in Christ Jesus for good works, which God prepared beforehand so that we would walk in them.

11 Therefore remember that formerly you, the Gentiles in the flesh, who are called "Uncircumcision" by the so-called "Circumcision," which is performed in the flesh by human hands—

12 remember that you were at that time separate from Christ, excluded from the commonwealth of Israel, and strangers to the covenants of promise, having no hope and without God in the world.

13 But now in Christ Jesus you who formerly were far off have been brought near by the blood of Christ.

14 For He Himself is our peace, who made both groups into one and broke down the barrier of the dividing wall,

15 by abolishing in His flesh the enmity, which is the Law of commandments contained in ordinances, so that in Himself He might make the two into one new man, thus establishing peace,

16 and might reconcile them both in one body to God through the cross, by it having put to death the enmity.

17 AND HE CAME AND PREACHED PEACE TO YOU WHO WERE FAR AWAY, AND PEACE TO THOSE WHO WERE NEAR;

18 for through Him we both have our access in one Spirit to the Father.

19   So then you are no longer strangers and aliens, but you are fellow citizens with the saints, and are of God's household,

20   having been built on the foundation of the apostles and prophets, Christ Jesus Himself being the corner stone,

21   in whom the whole building, being fitted together, is growing into a holy temple in the Lord,

21   in whom you also are being built together into a dwelling of God in the Spirit.

CHAPTER 3

1   For this reason I, Paul, the prisoner of Christ Jesus for the sake of you Gentiles—

2   if indeed you have heard of the stewardship of God's grace which was given to me for you;

3   that by revelation there was made known to me the mystery, as I wrote before in brief.

4   By referring to this, when you read you can understand my insight into the mystery of Christ,

5   which in other generations was not made known to the sons of men, as it has now been revealed to His holy apostles and prophets in the Spirit;

6   to be specific, that the Gentiles are fellow heirs and fellow members of the body, and fellow partakers of the promise in Christ Jesus through the gospel,

7   of which I was made a minister, according to the gift of God's grace which was given to me according to the working of His power.

8   To me, the very least of all saints, this grace was given, to preach to the Gentiles the unfathomable riches of Christ,

9   and to bring to light what is the administration of the mystery which for ages has been hidden in God who created all things;

10   so that the manifold wisdom of God might now be made known through the church to the rulers and the authorities in the heavenly places.

11   This was in accordance with the eternal purpose which He carried out in Christ Jesus our Lord,

12   in whom we have boldness and confident access through faith in Him.

13   Therefore I ask you not to lose heart at my tribulations on your behalf, for they are your glory.

14   For this reason I bow my knees before the Father,

15   from whom every family in heaven and on earth derives its name,

16   that He would grant you, according to the riches of His glory, to be strengthened with power through His Spirit in the inner man,

17   so that Christ may dwell in your hearts through faith; and that you, being rooted and grounded in love,

18   may be able to comprehend with all the saints what is the breadth and length and height and depth,

19   and to know the love of Christ which surpasses knowledge, that you may be filled

up to all the fullness of God.

20   Now to Him who is able to do far more abundantly beyond all that we ask or

think, according to the power that works within us,

21   to Him be the glory in the church and in Christ Jesus to all generations forever

and ever. Amen.

CHAPTER 4

1   Therefore I, the prisoner of the Lord, implore you to walk in a manner worthy of

the calling with which you have been called,

2   with all humility and gentleness, with patience, showing tolerance for one another

in love,

3   being diligent to preserve the unity of the Spirit in the bond of peace.

4   There is one body and one Spirit, just as also you were called in one hope of

your calling;

5   one Lord, one faith, one baptism,

6   one God and Father of all who is over all and through all and in all.

7   But to each one of us grace was given according to the measure of Christ's gift.

8   Therefore it says,

"WHEN HE ASCENDED ON HIGH,

HE LED CAPTIVE A HOST OF CAPTIVES,

AND HE GAVE GIFTS TO MEN."

9   (Now this expression, "He ascended," what does it mean except that He also had descended into the lower parts of the earth?

10   He who descended is Himself also He who ascended far above all the heavens, so that He might fill all things.)

11   And He gave some as apostles, and some as prophets, and some as evangelists, and some as pastors and teachers,

12   for the equipping of the saints for the work of service, to the building up of the body of Christ;

13   until we all attain to the unity of the faith, and of the knowledge of the Son of God, to a mature man, to the measure of the stature which belongs to the fullness of Christ.

14   As a result, we are no longer to be children, tossed here and there by waves and carried about by every wind of doctrine, by the trickery of men, by craftiness in deceitful scheming;

15   but speaking the truth in love, we are to grow up in all aspects into Him who is the head, even Christ,

16   from whom the whole body, being fitted and held together by what every joint supplies, according to the proper working of each individual part, causes the growth of the body for the building up of itself in love.

17   So this I say, and affirm together with the Lord, that you walk no longer just as the Gentiles also walk, in the futility of their mind,

18   being darkened in their understanding, excluded from the life of God because of

the ignorance that is in them, because of the hardness of their heart;

19   and they, having become callous, have given themselves over to the sensuality

for the practice of every kind of impurity with greediness.

20   But you did not learn Christ in this way,

21   if indeed you have heard Him and have been taught in Him, just as truth is

in Jesus,

22   that, in reference to your former manner of life, you lay aside the old self, which is

being corrupted in accordance with the lusts of deceit,

23   and that you be renewed in the spirit of your mind,

24   and put on the new self, which in the likeness of God has been created in

righteousness and holiness of the truth.

25   Therefore, laying aside falsehood, SPEAK TRUTH EACH ONE OF YOU WITH HIS

NEIGHBOR, for we are members of one another.

26   BE ANGRY, AND YET DO NOT SIN; do not let the sun go down on your anger,

27   and do not give the devil an opportunity.

28   He who steals must steal no longer; but rather he must labor, performing with his

own hands what is good, so that he will have something to share with one who

has need.

29   Let no unwholesome word proceed from your mouth, but only such a word as is

good for edification according to the need of the moment, so that it will give grace

to those who hear.

30   Do no grieve the Holy Spirit of God, by whom you were sealed for the day of

redemption.

31   Let all bitterness and wrath and anger and clamor and slander be put away from

you, along with all malice.

32   Be kind to one another, tender-hearted, forgiving each other, just as God in

Christ also has forgiven you.

CHAPTER 5_____

1   Therefore be imitators of God, as beloved children;

2   and walk in love, just as Christ also loved you and gave Himself up for us, an

offering and a sacrifice to God as a fragrant aroma.

3   But immorality or any impurity or greed must not even be named among you, as

is proper among saints;

4   and there must be no filthiness and silly talk, or coarse jesting, which are not

fitting, but rather giving of thanks.

5   For this you know with certainty, that no immoral or impure person or covetous

man, who is an idolater, has an inheritance in the kingdom of Christ and God.

6   Let no one deceive you with empty words, for because of these things the wrath

of God comes upon the sons of disobedience.

7   Therefore do not be partakers with them;

8   for you were formerly darkness, but now you are Light in the Lord; walk as

children of Light

9   (for the fruit of the Light consists in all goodness and righteousness and truth),

10   trying to learn what is pleasing to the Lord.

11   Do not participate in the unfruitful deeds of darkness, but instead even expose

them;

12   for it is disgraceful even to speak of the things which are done by them in secret.

13   But all things become visible when they are exposed by the light, for everything

that becomes visible is light.

14   For this reason it says,

"Awake, sleeper,

And arise from the dead,

And Christ will shine on you."

15   Therefore be careful how you walk, not as unwise men but as wise,

16   making the most of your time, because the days are evil.

17   So then do not be foolish, but understand what the will of the Lord is.

18   And do not get drunk with wine, for that is dissipation, but be filled with the Spirit,

19   speaking to one another in psalms and hymns and spiritual songs, singing and

making melody with your heart to the Lord;

20   always giving thanks for all things in the name of our Lord Jesus Christ to God,

even the Father;

21   and be subject to one another in the fear of Christ.

22   Wives, be subject to your own husbands, as to the Lord.

23   For the husband is the head of the wife, as Christ also is the head of the church,

He Himself being the Savior of the body.

24 But as the church is subject to Christ, so also the wives ought to be to their husbands in everything.

25 Husbands, love your wives, just as Christ also loved the church and gave Himself up for her,

26 so that He might sanctify her, having cleansed her by the washing of water with the word,

27 that He might present to Himself the church in all her glory, having no spot or wrinkle or any such thing; but that she would be holy and blameless.

28 So husbands ought to love their own wives as their own bodies. He who loves his own wife loves himself;

29 for no one ever hated his own flesh, but nourishes and cherishes it, just as Christ also does the church,

30 because we are members of His body.

31 FOR THIS REASON A MAN SHALL LEAVE HIS FATHER AND MOTHER AND SHALL BE JOINED TO HIS WIFE, AND THE TWO SHALL BECOME ONE FLESH.

32 This mystery is great; but I am speaking with reference to Christ and the church.

33 Nevertheless, each individual among you also is to love his own wife even as himself, and the wife must see to it that she respects her husband.

CHAPTER 6_____

1 Children, obey your parents in the Lord, for this is right.

2 HONOR YOUR FATHER AND MOTHER (which is the first commandment with a promise),

3 SO THAT IT MAY BE WELL WITH YOU, AND THAT YOU MAY LIVE LONG ON THE EARTH.

4   Fathers, do not provoke your children to anger, but bring them up in the discipline and instruction of the Lord.

5   Slaves, be obedient to those who are your masters according to the flesh, with fear and trembling, in the sincerity of your heart, as to Christ;

6   not by way of eyeservice, as men-pleasers, but as slaves of Christ, doing the will of God from the heart.

7   With good will render service, as to the Lord, and not to men,

8   knowing that whatever good thing each one does, this he will receive back from the Lord, whether slave or free.

9   And masters, do the same things to them, and give up threatening, knowing that both their Master and yours is in heaven, and there is no partiality with Him.

10   Finally, be strong in the Lord and in the strength of His might.

11   Put on the full armor of God, so that you will be able to stand firm against the schemes of the devil.

12   For our struggle is not against flesh and blood, but against the rulers, against the powers, against the world forces of this darkness, against the spiritual forces of wickedness in the heavenly places.

13   Therefore, take up the full armor of God, so that you will be able to resist in the evil day, and having done everything, to stand firm.

14   Stand firm therefore, HAVING GIRDED YOUR LOINS WITH TRUTH, AND HAVING PUT ON THE BREASTPLATE OF RIGHTEOUSNESS,

15   and having shod YOUR FEET WITH THE PREPARTION OF THE GOSPEL OF PEACE;

16   in addition to all, taking up the shield of faith with which you will be able to extinguish all the flaming arrows of the evil one.

17   And take THE HELMET OF SALVATION, and the sword of the Spirit, which is the word of God.

18   With all prayer and petition pray at all times in the Spirit, and with this in view, be on the alert with all perseverance and petition for all the saints,

19   and pray on my behalf, that utterance may be given to me in the opening of my mouth, to make known with boldness the mystery of the gospel,

20   for which I am an ambassador in chains; that in proclaiming it I may speak boldly, as I ought to speak.

21   verse 21 omitted (See Bible)

22   verse 22 omitted (See Bible)

23   Peace be to the brethren, and love with faith, from God the Father and the Lord Jesus Christ.

24   Grace be with all those who love our Lord Jesus Christ with incorruptible love.

GLOSSARY OF WORDS

These words are definitions found by the Strong's number in *The Complete Word Study, New Testament*, by Dr. Zodhiates.

WEEK 2

Adoption (5206)—to receive another into the relationship of child, belonging to God; this word illustrates the greatness of divine love in making a stranger, such as a sinner, to be a real son/daughter

Redemption (629)—to release on payment of ransom; a price paid; redeem

Sealed (4972)—to stamp with a signet ring or private mark for security and preservation

Pledge (728)—earnest money; something that stands for part of the price and paid beforehand to confirm a bargain; Holy Spirit given here on earth to assure a believer of their future and eternal inheritance

WEEK 3

Wisdom (4678)—the knowledge of how to regulate one's relationship with God

Revelation (602)—uncovering; unveiling; disclosure

Knowledge (1922)—clear and exact knowledge; knowledge with very powerful influences, very personal

Heart (1271)—understanding; mind; an operation of the understanding of thought

Enlightened (5461)—to give light in a spiritual sense; to make to see or understand; to bring to light

Hope (1680)—desire of some good with expectation of obtaining it; trust; confidence in someone

Calling (2821)—a calling; condition; or employment

Riches (4149)—wealth; abundance; valuable bestowment; fullness

Glory (1391)—to recognize a person for what they are; reputation; honor; appearance; form commanding attention

Exceeding (5235)—to throw beyond the usual mark; to surpass

Power (1411)—being able; capable; one who has the ability

Accordance (2596)—with the primary meaning of down; down from; used of place indicating motion down from a higher to a lower place

WEEK 4

Grace (5485)—favor; kindness granted; a benefit; unearned favor; undeserved favor; unmerited favor

Sanctify (37)—to hallow; set apart; withdraw from fellowship with the world by first gaining fellowship with God

WEEK 5

Peace (1515)—rest; absence or end of strife; a state of untroubled, undisturbed well-being

WEEK 6

Mystery (3466)—something hidden until revealed

WEEK 7

Lose heart (1573)—to be weak; to faint; fail in heart

Strengthen (2901)—to empower; increase in vigor

Power (1411)—being able; capable; one who has the ability

Dwell (2730)—refers to a certain fixed and durable dwelling; habitation

Grounded (2311)—to lay a basis for; erect; consolidated

Comprehend (2638)—to take; to seize; lay hold of; apprehend in a figurative sense

Know (1097)—usually to know experientially; to know and understand

Filled (4137)—to fill, as a net with fish or the smell of perfume in a house; to fill up and supply

WEEK 8

Implore (3870)—by the side of; to call to one's side, hence aid; to try to obtain by asking

Walk (4043)—to tread around; walk at large; companion with; follow; be occupied with

Worthy (516)—appropriately; after a godly sort; as becomes something/to liken

Unity (1775)—oneness; unanimity

One (1520))—means one numerically

Supplies (2024)—contribution; supply; to furnish besides; aid; fully supply

Proper working (1753)—efficiently; energy; operation; effectual working

WEEK 9

Lay aside (659)—to put away; cast off; lay down

Renewed (365)—to renew; make young; to be renewed insofar as a spiritual vitality is concerned; qualitatively new

Put on (1746)—in the sense of sinking into a garment; to invest with clothing

Grieve (3076)—to sorrow; to cause to grieve inward; to crowd into a narrow space or push into the corner

WEEK 10

Imitators (3042)—follower; an imitator, from "to mimic"

Partaker (4830)—co-participant; denotes union or together with

Light (5457)—like light of the sun or day; it is never kindled and therefore never quenched

WEEK 11

Carefully (199)—exactly; circumspectly; diligently; from "most exact"

Wise (4680)—signifies watchman; one who knows how to regulate his course in view of God's movements

Making the most (1805)—to buy or redeem from; to buy up; not allowing a suitable moment to pass by unheeded

Filled (4137)—to fill, as a net with fish or smell of perfume in a house; to fill up and supply

Be subject (5293)—put under; to order; to place in an orderly fashion under something

WEEK 12

Strong (1743)—to strengthen; to make strong; vigorous; become strong

In (1722)—a primary idea of rest in or on a thing; remaining in

Power (2904)—to hold fast; force; manifested power and dominion

Put on (1746)—in the sense of sinking into a garment; to invest with clothing

Stand (2476)—to set; place; to remain; abide; continue; to stand still; establish

Schemes (3180)—methods; the following or pursuing of orderly and technical procedures in the handling of a subject; to systematically work

Resist (436)—to stand against; oppose; withstand

Done (2716)—to work fully; accomplish; to finish or fashion

WEEK 13

Shield (2375)—a large door-shaped shield

Made in the USA
San Bernardino, CA
25 January 2017